WHEN JESUS WINS YOUR
HUSBAND'S HEART

WHEN JESUS WINS
YOUR
HUSBAND'S HEART

Lynn Forrester

Eagle

Trowbridge

Terra Nova Publications

First published by Eagle Publishing Ltd, 2002
Terra Nova Publications Ltd, 2002

Published in Great Britain by
Eagle Publishing Ltd
6 Kestrel House, Mill Street, Trowbridge, Wiltshire BA14 8BE
and
Terra Nova Publications Ltd
PO Box 2400, Bradford on Avon, Wiltshire BA15 2YN

ISBN 0 86347 567 1 [Eagle]

ISBN 1 90194 917 6 [Terra Nova]

Printed in Malta by Gutenberg Press

Contents

Dedication

With my love, and God's richest blessings,

*to the wonderful men and women who have allowed
me to share the most intimate and personal details
of their lives, in the knowledge that it is God's desire
to bless others as he has blessed them;*

*to the many people who have prayed with and for us
over the years —I could not have done it without you;*

*to my mum and dad and sister Maureen, who listened to me
when I told them about Jesus, thereby giving me hope that,
'You and your household will be saved';*

*to my husband Robert, my friend, my love, and now my
soulmate: you have given me so much —thank you for
believing I could write this book. The best is yet to come!*

Above all:

*All honour, praise and glory belongs to the Lord.
Thank you, heavenly Father, not only for answering
my prayers for my husband, but for giving me
far more than I ever dreamed possible.*

Lynn Forrester

Foreword

by

Mark Bailey

Vicar of Holy Trinity Church, Cheltenham
Member of New Wine Leadership Team

It may seem obvious to say this, but God has a very high view of marriage! His purpose for marriage is that husband and wife become soul mates. He wants couples to be joined at a level of being that goes beyond their bodies, intellects, finances and circumstances. God wants two people, who are very different, to be joined together at the level of their spirits, so that they share the deepest kind of intimacy; and so that they reflect more of the love of God, the Holy Trinity. This kind of spiritual inter-dependence can only be enjoyed when husband and wife are both filled with the Spirit of God.

It comes as no surprise, therefore, to know that there is a terrible ache in the heart, a loneliness that cannot be described, when, as a wife, you are unable to share the deepest part of your being with your husband; when your spouse is unable to understand or share in your ultimate hopes and dreams and goals. It is so difficult to build and plan for the future when both of you have different starting points.

This has been the past experience — the loneliness, the sadness, the pain — of Lynn Forrester's life. It is an experience that countless numbers of other women have gone through and are going through. Lynn, however, never gave up! She never stopped hoping, praying and believing, that one day her husband Rob would find God, and that they would be able to share together at even the deepest level of spiritual intimacy.

It has been a delight and joy to welcome Lynn and Rob into the family here at Trinity. Their story of how they came to be able to share in a faith in Christ together has been a great blessing to many of us, and a great encouragement. Their story, along with many other stories in this book, will encourage you if you find that your husband has not yet come through to faith. It will encourage you to keep loving your husband, praying in faith, and hoping for the future.

In the midst of much gloom and doom, it is so exciting and refreshing to hear of these real life stories of couples eventually coming together in Christ Jesus —some spectacular, others not so spectacular, all over different periods of time. For those who are wavering and discouraged, allow this book to encourage your faith in the living God, strengthen you in the faith that you have, to keep praying for your loved ones to come to Jesus. This is a great book, and reminds us that the same God who came to earth as Jesus Christ, two thousand years ago, is still at work today!

Introduction

"Believe in the Lord Jesus, and you will be saved
—you and your household."

Acts 16:31

When Jesus Wins Your Husband's Heart is a collection of stories of ordinary men who have had extra-ordinary conversions to Christianity. The exciting thing about each testimony is that behind every saved man was a praying woman. Ordinary women, many of whom had given their husbands the shock of their lives by announcing they had become Christians, decided to hold God to his word and claim their husbands in prayer. Each story is unique, but one fact is evident in all of them. The men all put up a pretty impressive fight: each man dared to wrestle with God —and 'lost' (but, in reality, gained everything!) I believe that the prayers of their wives weakened their desire and ability to resist God.

Whether your husband is vehemently opposed to your faith, tolerant or indifferent—take heart that God has his almighty hand on him. In Acts 16, we read of the jailer who asked Paul and Silas, "What must I do to be saved?"

Paul replied, **"Believe in the Lord Jesus and you will be saved – you and your household."** When I first read that verse, I saw it as a direct promise from the throne of God for my family. I had already fulfilled it in part by becoming a believer myself; now, I started living in faith for my household.

Within two years, both my parents, my sister, brother-in-law, their three children and an aunt and uncle were all believers! I had no doubt at all that God was indeed true to his word, so I turned my prayer attention to my husband.

Since I started to write this book, many women have queued up to tell me about their husband's conversion. I could write reams of success stories, but instead I have chosen just six. Each reflects a person from a different walk of life; here are ordinary men and women who now have an extraordinary faith in Jesus Christ.

God is in the business of saving husbands. One woman told me that her husband, a university lecturer, was so confident that God did not exist that she actually started doubting her own faith. That was until one day when she fell on her knees before God, and he led her to Luke 13:6. This is the parable of the fig tree that did not bear fruit for three years. Eventually, the owner said to the gardener, "Cut it down! Why should it use up the soil?" But the gardener was horrified, and asked for a reprieve for the tree because he knew that, given the right care, it would once again bear fruit. The owner agreed, so the gardener dug around the roots of the tree, applied fertiliser and tended the tree so that it would bear fruit the following year. When she read that parable, she knew in her heart that she should dig around the roots of her husband's unbelief for one year, and wait for God to bear fruit at the end of that time. So, for a whole year, she interceded for her husband with prayer and blessings. Every day, for 365 days and nights, she called out to God for her husband's salvation, always bearing in mind that the tree in the parable was expected to bear fruit. On the last day of her vigil, totally unaware of his wife's labours, her husband came before God and gave his heart to the Lord. What an amazing God we have.

I met a woman whose husband, throughout their forty year marriage, could not see the point of asking Jesus into his life. He was happy for his wife to go to church, but remained disinterested throughout their marriage. He developed cancer and, throughout the time of his illness and treatment, still refused to accept Jesus into his life. However, a few hours before he died, he told his wife he was ready to put his life right with God, and accept Jesus as his Saviour. She led him through the prayer of commitment four hours before he died. This is not to encourage anyone to delay receiving Jesus; it simply reminds us that we must never give up, never stop praying, for as long as a spouse lives.

Another woman told me that, after nearly thirty years of marriage, her lawyer husband 'went into shock' after she became a Christian. She told me that she soon became used to his "sharp words and anger" towards her, but she decided that his behaviour was not God's best plan for their lives, so she met with friends weekly, and called out continuously to God to change her husband's attitude towards her and Jesus. She never in her wildest dreams imagined how God would answer her prayers. One day, as her husband was rushing to get ready for a business meeting, he could not find his tie pin and was irritated by its disappearance. Noticing a small crucifix pin sitting on his wife's dressing table, and as he was in a hurry, he decided to use it to keep his tie in place. He left the house, upset and irritable, and went off to his business meeting. During lunch, a fellow businessman leaned across the table and asked him, "Does that cross mean anything to you, or is it just to keep your tie tidy?" There was not a great deal of business discussed during that meeting; and by the end of the lunch, the woman's husband had asked the Lord into his life. He was converted at the dining table by a man he had never met before, who had simply noticed his tiepin and taken it as a God-given opportunity to reach out to him. Needless to say, she had the shock of her life when he came home. In her own words, she said, "My husband came home a new man; he even looked different."

I believe, with all my heart, that no one is too tough, angry, intellectual or stubborn for Jesus. If Jesus can melt our husbands' hearts, he can melt your husband's, too. God has no favourites; we are no more special to Jesus than you are. We are not spiritual giants; we are ordinary women, who learnt how to pray and believe that: **"You and your household"** will be saved.

My prayer is that this book offers you hope and encouragement, to enable you to intercede for your husband. I look forward to hearing about your husband's conversion. Enjoy the journey peacefully, and never lose sight of the fact that, when Jesus wins your husband's heart, you will have an amazing story to tell. You never know, we might just read about you both in *When Jesus Wins Your Husband's Heart, Book Two*!

Lynn Forrester

1

Robert Forrester

**"As a scientist I could not prove the existence of God;
therefore he did not exist. How wrong could I be!"**

As a boy, I attended church often with my parents and felt I
knew a lot about religion. Church had little to offer me; it was
more about what I could *not* do than what I could. Services
were dull and lifeless, and by the time I was eighteen I could
not wait to get away from the restrictions of home and church.
I was offered a place at Edinburgh University to study
medicine, and set off for Scotland with great excitement, to
start my new life.

My first year at university was quite miserable for
me. I was in awful lodgings, half starving and freezing cold
for most of the time. God certainly was nowhere to be
seen. I felt homesick, and struggled to cope without the
comforts of home. I dealt with this by throwing myself into
student life. Bars, concerts, plays and parties became my
home, and I soon made friends with people who felt no need
of God. I made a conscious decision to abandon my
childhood religious teaching and concentrate on widening my
knowledge of philosophy, politics and the arts, as was the

trend at that time. As far as I was concerned, Christianity was opium for the masses: one enormous global con trick; and it was time to leave my childhood behind.

At that time in my life, I was unable to believe and accept many things in the Bible. I could not accept that Jesus was the Son of God; and I had huge problems with, for example, the story of the wise men following the star. Physics seemed to dictate that if the wise men came from the east and followed a star, they would simply have gone around in circles, ending up where they started. Another big issue for me was why the Jews were unprepared for Jesus' birth. They were waiting for their Messiah, yet seemed, to me, not to have a clue about what was going on. I understood little of these things, so it just did not seem to make sense. I did not accept the Bible as a true account. The whole foundation of Christianity seemed then to be contradictory, and I could not 'buy into' something I thought to be mistaken.

I thoroughly enjoyed my studies at Edinburgh, and liked the precise, logical order of science; it reinforced my belief that Christianity was opium for the masses. As a scientist, I could not prove the existence of God: therefore, he did not exist. That was my state of mind. For the next decade, I had no reason to think about my decision again. I qualified as a doctor, and embarked on a career in medicine.

When I was twenty six years old, and working as a surgical registrar, I met my wife, Lynn. Our courtship was great fun and exciting. Like me, she was not at all interested in religion, but we did decide to marry in a church, simply because it was the 'done thing'. For me, the service carried no implication of a religious commitment, merely a social and moral one.

We soon settled down into married life, and moved to Jersey for a three month surgical registrar locum. I had been working in London and was absolutely exhausted, so three months in the sunshine seemed very appealing. Sadly, a few days after we arrived in Jersey, I heard the news that my father had died of a massive heart attack. I was mortified and, for a long time, could not come to terms with his death, becoming withdrawn and drinking too much. Lynn started going to church, but I did not really think much about it as I was so engrossed in my own grief. My feeling was that she would soon grow bored with church.

However, several months later, as I emerged from my grief, I was shocked to discover that Lynn was serious about religion. In fact, she told me she believed in Jesus and was "a born again Christian".

I was dumbfounded. How could my beautiful, intelligent wife believe in a load of nonsense? It was beyond me. I argued with her that God did not—could not—exist, but she was adamant that she was right and I was wrong. I felt confident that she would soon become disillusioned and give it all up. I was content to let her get on with it —for now.

With the passage of time, it dawned on me that her interest was not fading as I had expected. She was fully engrossed in the church. She read endless Christian books and played Christian music all the time. Suddenly, her whole life was dominated by religion. My irritation soon turned to outright anger. I had Jesus crammed down my throat constantly. Christian books, music, notes and Bibles littered our home. I could not stand the intensity of her relationship with God, nor the fact that she was forcing me to address issues I had long since abandoned. I had not thought about God for nearly a decade, and resented being forced to go along paths I had already trodden and rejected.

In some way that I cannot really describe very well, I was jealous of the time and attention Lynn gave God. If she had come home and told me she had fallen in love with another man, I could have done something about that. But this Jesus was something else; I had no course of redress. I had an unseen, unreachable rival that I truly believed was a figment of the imagination. Lynn had fallen for the biggest con in creation and I was powerless to stop what was happening.

I tried to reason with her, but she was adamant: as far as she was concerned, God was for real. Jesus was the Son of God, who had died for our sins, and the Holy Spirit was sent to guide and teach us. I was so concerned that Lynn was getting involved with some sort of cult that I went along to church with her, to find out what was going on. I was surprised to find a traditional Anglican church. The service was 'happy clappy', but fairly harmless until someone stood up and started speaking in tongues. I was very uncomfortable with that. Sensitive to my discomfort, Lynn whisked me away after the service. Suddenly, someone from the church (a visitor, as it happened) raced after us, stopped us in the middle of the high street, and harangued Lynn for being ashamed of her faith! He bombarded her with scripture, then released us from his grip and turned on his heels. We went home in shock. Lynn was highly embarrassed, and I was even more determined to get her out of the church.

By this time I had signed a permanent job contract, and we were set to stay in Jersey for a year or two. People from the church started to invite us to their homes. I remember one particular occasion being invited out on someone's sailing boat, when I was 'Bible bashed' for several hours, with no form of escape. It was torture! I cannot understand why we accepted the invitation, as I could not swim at the time, and Lynn suffers from sea sickness! Show Lynn a boat, and she immediately reaches for the anti-seasickness tablets, sprawls on deck and prays for an end to the suffering! We headed out into Gorey bay, threw out a few fishing lines, and waited for the fish to bite. Someone referred to the fact that Jesus liked to hang out with fishermen, and I knew in an instant I was in for a sermon. I was like a rat in a trap. I was tempted to hurl myself into the water and take my chances! Lynn's *mal de mer* was not miraculously cured, and she spent most of the journey 'laying ground bait' for the fish. For two long hours I wished I could escape!

The invitations rolled in: more acceptances; more endless Bible bashing. Everyone seemed to think that I had neither heard who Jesus was, nor understood I had a choice to make. It was beyond their comprehension that I had made my choice to say 'no', and that I did not want to be converted. Lynn and I would often argue after each social occasion. I just could not relax with her friends, and decided I would rather stay at home. Looking back, I realise that I have probably missed out on some wonderful friendships because of my prejudice.

Eventually, our children were born and we settled into family life. We discussed everything barring religion. Our first child was christened, but only because it was the done thing in our family; it meant nothing to me. Lynn initially took the children to church with her. Whilst they were young this did not matter too much to me but, as they grew up and started talking about Jesus, I began to object to their religious indoctrination. I felt the children should be left to make up their own minds as adults. I told Lynn she could not take the children to church any more.

Lynn was an excellent mother. She was so loving and always knew how to handle the children and bring out the best in them. I, on the other hand, struggled hugely; I barely coped with the children. Lynn would go to church on her own, but in time she became tired of returning home to two unhappy children and a fraught husband. She eventually gave up church herself, which suited me fine. I thought it would only be a matter of time for her to get this 'God stuff' out of her system. It soon became apparent though that Lynn continued with her faith. She would still read her Bible, and all her Christian paraphernalia was moved into her car. I occasionally heard her praying with the children at bedtime, but chose to ignore that one.

In 1989, Lynn invited me to an FGBMFI (Full Gospel Businessmen's Fellowship International) dinner. At the time, I was having a few problems with an eye disorder. As the speaker was a retired eye surgeon, she thought I might relate to his testimony. I think she probably thought I was going to be miraculously healed and converted, all in one go. I agreed to go with her, simply because I could see how much it meant to her. We went along to a local hotel for dinner. I was horrified that no sooner had we sat down than people started to sing songs and worship Jesus. They behaved as if they were in a 'happy clappy' church. I nearly died of embarrassment. One woman kept holding her arms up to the ceiling and shouting, "Praise you Jesus." I was mortified! The whole evening was excruciatingly painful and I could barely bring myself to look up from my plate, never mind hold a conversation with anyone. I do not think I heard a word the speaker said; all I wanted to do was get out of the place. I felt trapped and extremely embarrassed. I was furious, and unleashed the full force of my wrath, telling Lynn in no uncertain terms not to expect me to go with her to anything like that again.

Whenever Lynn referred to Christianity, I would instantly become hostile and aggressive. I believed that I had let her down as a husband in order for her to believe in a fairy tale. I felt frustrated and angry with this non-existent God of hers. I had made a decision years before to abandon God, but now my wife was forcing me to think about issues I had buried long ago. The closer she was to God, the more hostile I became.

Despite our opposing views of Christianity, we somehow managed to have a good marriage together. Without doubt, Lynn was the best thing that had happened to me—she was so much a part of me that I did not know where I started and she finished. We enjoyed each other's company, and laughed a lot together. But as her faith drove me to distraction, I resolved to ignore it as far as possible.

After a couple of years, I moved from the hospital into general practice. The medical system in Jersey is quite different from that of the UK. Whilst hospital treatment is free, visits to the general practitioner are not. I found the private system difficult. I was not very good at asking people to pay for medical care, especially if they were not very well off. I was not a businessman, and felt a conflict between my vocational role and my need to provide financially for my family. I think it is fair to say that I was hugely influenced by the affluent lifestyles so many people enjoyed in Jersey. I wanted to be wealthy, and I certainly was not going to make my fortune in medicine. I struggled in general practice for ten years, until finally I became disillusioned with medicine and was restless for a change of career.

I had been dabbling in the commodity market for some

time, with some success, and decided to make it my full time job. The only way I could do that was to sell my practice and invest the proceeds from the sale. Lynn was supportive and agreed to my venture, providing I agreed to certain conditions. The first was that I would write to the General Medical Council and apply for my vocational practice certificate, which would allow me to return to work as a GP in the UK without further training. The second was that I would not fall below a certain amount of money, so that we could restart; and the third was that I would tell her if things were going wrong. I readily agreed to her conditions, never for one moment thinking that I could fail.

So, in the summer of 1993, I gave up general practice and started trading the commodity market. I threw myself into my new role, and surrounded myself with the trappings of success. I bought a top of the range computer, mobile phone and fax, and began trading the commodity markets. I lasted five months, and lost every penny we had. Everything we had worked for over the years was gone almost overnight. Events moved quickly, and I rapidly spiralled into a huge amount of debt. I was devastated, and could not think how to tell Lynn. Not only was our financial loss enormous, but I had not kept my promises to her. There were no safety nets in place as I had agreed. I had not contacted the GMC; I had not let her know things were going wrong, and I had not kept a financial reserve for a restart. I knew I had failed her big time, and could not imagine why she would want to stay with me after I had let her down so badly. Telling her what I had done was one of the hardest things I have ever had to do in my life.

Once the enormity of what I had done hit me, I deteriorated into a mass of self pity and shock. Lynn rallied round, and was determined to keep our family together. We were propelled into an alien financial world, made bearable by the support of loving friends. Lynn was amazingly supportive and was a great tower of strength. I still failed to recognise where her strength came from; looking back, I can see God had his hand firmly upon us. The following weeks were hellish, and six months later we were forced to relocate. We avoided bankruptcy by the skin of our teeth, and I managed to get a job as a doctor in the UK, in a private clinic.

Lynn had a good job in Jersey. She was content and very happy, and I had to tear her away from everything and everyone she loved. I know it was an extremely painful time for her. Throughout this time she was amazingly supportive, never once accusing me of letting her down, either verbally or in her manner. She simply kept telling me that God would look after us. I never believed her, and knew I had a hard job ahead of me to rebuild our lives.

However, there was one major change in store for me. Lynn told me she had had enough of my anti-Christian behaviour. She explained that she could not get through our problems without Jesus, and that, if we were to make a go of our marriage, I had to change my attitude towards her faith. She was tired of being persecuted in her own home, and would not stand for any more ear bashings, or being forbidden by me to go to church. If I could not accept her for who she was, then I could divorce her. I was terrified at the thought of losing her, and knew that plenty of other women would have divorced me for what I had done. I was so grateful that she still wanted to stay with me that I did not put up a fight. I expected her to go on a Christianity frenzy, but she did not. She went to church regularly and attended a ladies' prayer group once a week but, apart from that, our home life did not change at all. I had little to complain about.

By this time, the children had started a new school and were finding the change difficult to cope with. We could see them dissolve into unhappy, under-confident youngsters. It became apparent that we needed to move them to a different school. Lynn said she would pray about the situation. As usual, she prayed and I worried. We went to look at Dean Close School in Cheltenham. I warmed to the headmaster immediately —despite the fact that he was a Christian. I knew that I had to put the children's needs before my own prejudice, so found myself agreeing to send them to a Christian school. Trusting that they would make their own decisions about God when they were older, as I had done, I agreed they could start at Dean Close. My priority was to restore their confidence and happiness, not to 'Christian bash'. Because the school was thirty miles away, we needed to move house, which led us onto another major event in our lives. When we left Jersey, we did not have a penny to our names, only a mountain of debt. Now, seven years on, we are solvent. God did that in an amazing way. A year after returning to England, I was left some money in my aunt's will. It enabled us to put a deposit on a house, allowing us to get out of the rent trap. We scoured the county, looking for a house we could afford and that we all liked. We went out every weekend, looking at properties, with two unhappy children in the back of the car. I first saw Orchard House on a gloomy, early spring day. It was empty, and we roamed from room to room. Lynn really did not like the house at all, but I did. The children were fed up with travelling so far to school every day, and were desperate to settle. Though at that time it was neglected, the house had obviously once had a well loved and tended garden, complete with vegetable patch and greenhouse. I was sure we could soon settle in and sort out the place. By some miracle, we were offered a mortgage, and things looked set to move quickly. We were told that the house was in trust to a bank, following the death of the owner, and assumed he had been an old man. It took several months to exchange contracts on the empty house, and we could not understand why things were taking so long to progress. Eventually, we agreed a contract date, and looked forward to moving in at long last. The night before we were due to sign the contracts, Lynn had a telephone call from someone who lived in the village to which we were moving, who had heard that we were buying Orchard House. The caller asked if we knew who had lived in the house previously, and she then told us that an entire family who had lived there had died in the most tragic and distressing circumstances. We were both so upset. Our hearts ached for the relatives of those who had died. We discussed how we felt about going to live in a house with such a tragic past. As far as I was concerned, what was past was past. I was neither superstitious nor religious, so my response was quite philosophical: it was just a house; we liked it, and wanted to buy it, so nothing had changed for me. Knowing what had happened would make no difference to my life. Lynn's attitude was quite different. She explained that she could only live in the house if it had some sort of a Christian blessing before we moved in. She felt that something very evil and abnormal had happened in that place, and that it needed to be cleansed. I said that was fine by me, as long as I was not expected to be involved.

It was obviously very important that our children would be happy in our new home, and we were honest with them about the tragic deaths we had heard about. We discussed what the local people might think about the house: that they might think it was a frightening place to live in. Unbeknown to me, Lynn had prayed with the children, and had asked Jesus to make Orchard House a happy place again. We were all in agreement that we wanted to live there.

A few months after moving, another crisis hit us. By this time I was getting used to things not running smoothly! Once again, I had to go home and tell Lynn we were heading for stormy waters. Things were so tight financially that we could have lost the house. Lynn was firm in her faith, and I remember her saying, "God hasn't brought us to this house for us to leave in disgrace. He'll sort it out!" By this time I was retraining as a GP and had taken a huge drop in income and we had amassed debt from my commodity fiasco. On top of this, I now had to employ a lawyer to sort out yet another problem, and had legal fees to find, as we found that we did not qualify for legal aid. I managed to persuade the bank to lend me £5,000 for legal costs, hoping the matter would be resolved before more money was needed. Lynn was quick to mention that God would look after us, and that she would be praying into the situation. I still had no faith in her God, and resolved to, somehow, sort out the problem myself. Lynn tried to persuade me to ask God to help us, but I would not budge, saying that it was a pointless exercise. She eventually begged me to read a copy of *Why Jesus?* and to say one prayer. She said that, if I did so, she would promise never again to ask me to pray. I thought that was a fairly good deal, and agreed, just to pacify her. I was not impressed with the *Why Jesus?* booklet, and the short prayer seemed harmless enough. I could not then have known what an impact it would have upon my life:

> "God, I don't believe in you,
> but if you are there, show me. Amen"

An incredible chain of events took place, following that prayer. Our financial situation worsened. We were desperate to get the case resolved, so that I could meet my financial commitments. Then, amazingly, our lawyer offered to continue to work on the case without payment. I could scarcely believe it! Lynn was convinced it was an answer to prayer. I had no idea then that the dispute would take another year to settle. Eventually, we did get everything that I was owed, and the legal fees, which came to the staggering sum of £45,000, were paid for by the other party. We could never have afforded to continue with the case from our own resources. The crisis was happily past, but, as far as I was concerned at that time, it was resolved in my own strength, not God's. I can scarcely believe that I was so naive and conceited.

Then another amazing thing happened. Our house had a large garden, which we found difficult to keep up. A local builder knocked on the door and asked if we would like to sell our garden as a building plot, making us an offer we could not refuse. With the proceeds of the sale, we were able to transform the house completely. We have been incredibly happy here, and now I am amazed at the blessings God has heaped upon us —all because Lynn honoured him, and never wavered in her faith.

During that time, I worked alternate weeks as a resident medical officer in a private hospital whilst I did my general practice training on the other weeks. This meant spending fourteen days and nights a month away from home. The work was demanding during daylight hours, but the evenings were long and lonely. One evening, I was especially bored, having just finished my copy of *Moby Dick*; the televised cricket had been cancelled, due to poor weather; and the wards were quiet—so I had time on my hands. Mooching around the flat, I looked for something to read, eventually finding a Gideon's Bible and a Jeffrey Archer novel. No contest—the Bible won. I thought: what the heck, let me prove Lynn wrong! I decided that I would prove once and for all that the Bible was a load of rubbish, and that God did not exist. I decided to read the Gospels first, since that is where Jesus makes his appearance in the world. That night, and for weeks afterwards, I searched for loopholes, realising that I had never really read the Bible before. I was amazed to discover that one of the first miracles recorded was Jesus turning water into wine. So he was not a killjoy, after all! Certainly, this was a far cry from the teetotal message I had heard in the Church of Scotland services I attended as a boy.

I read the Gospels several times and, as I was not getting very far with my plan to find loopholes, decided to try another version of the Bible. Had the 'lies' been lost in translation? I remembered an old King James Bible I had bought as a teenager, which had been collecting dust for years. Perhaps that version would reveal the truth. So I started to take the Bible to the hospital with me—and found that I enjoyed reading it. I was a man on a mission, determined to prove to Lynn that God did not exist. Eventually, Lynn noticed I had removed the Bible from our bedroom, and she asked me about it. I was furious. I had been rumbled, so I grunted something about it making a good paperweight. I did not want her to ask me about it. When I could prove that God did not exist, I would then tell her what I had been working on for so many weeks.

Towards the millennium, *The Daily Telegraph* started printing tokens to collect, for copies of the New Testament that were being given away. I found myself cutting out the coupons and sending off for them. I secretly read them from cover to cover, several times, still searching for loopholes. At the same time, a series of articles on the history of Christianity was published, and I devoured these, too. They were so interesting. I started to read information I had not explored before. As I was still not getting very far with pulling the Bible to pieces, I started to ask Lynn questions about God, hoping to catch her out. She would answer gently and confidently. If she did not know the answer to my question, she always found out. She kept referring to Jesus and the Holy Spirit as though they were real persons. This was a new concept to me. She patiently told me more about the personality of the Trinity. She maintained that I had known religion as a boy, but not a personal relationship with the Lord. At the time, I did not know what she meant. I do now.

Eventually, I started work as a general practitioner in Swindon, and began to be struck by the number of people who came into my surgery with their lives in a mess. A small proportion of my patients had genuine medical problems, but the majority were suffering from depression. Marital breakdowns, adultery, terminations, incest, divorce, substance abuse: all these things seemed to be tearing people's lives apart. I started to wonder why the fabric of society was breaking down, and became aware that there was a moral gap in people's lives, which was being filled by things that initially brought pleasure, but which were soon replaced by long term pain.

I realise now that Jesus was revealing himself to me in so many ways. I usually finished work early on a Wednesday, and enjoyed listening to the radio on my way home. I was surprised to tune in to a broadcast of choral evensong, as I thought such services had long since ceased. On one occasion, I started to listen to a breathtakingly beautiful rendition of a psalm. It was angelic, and I found myself moved by the music and listening to the readings. As I was still on a mission to prove to Lynn that God did not exist, I continued to listen. Evensong became a regular Wednesday habit for me —in the interests of research!

We started to put down roots. We were living in a beautiful part of the country, and life was good for us. However, I found myself wondering whether this was as a result of my efforts or Lynn's prayers. I started to entertain the thought that it was probably the latter, but kept that thought a closely guarded secret!

Some time later, the *Daily Telegraph* reviewed a book based on the story of the three wise men travelling to find Jesus. An astronomer, who also happened to have an interest in coin collecting, had found a coin minted in Syria in 100AD, which bore a picture of a ram and a star. Using a computer, he was able to establish what would have been the visible position of the stars and planets in the period immediately before Jesus' birth, and discovered that Jupiter, Saturn and the moon were all together in a particular, recognizable juxtaposition at that time. Contrary to the belief I had held, the men from the east did not follow a single star and go round in circles. They were following a planetary alignment which led them straight into Bethlehem. The 'wise men' were keen observers of the movements of heavenly objects; it was part of their culture, but not Jewish culture. At last, a major biblical event made sense to me.

Soon afterwards, my mother became ill, and it was a particularly sad time for me. Although I was a doctor, I could do little to help her. There were times we would visit and she would be as sweet as pie. On other visits, she was aggressive, and convinced we were trying to harm her or take her money. I had seen this pattern many times as a doctor, but it was so difficult to deal with on a personal level. Finally, she became so ill that she was admitted to hospital. The night she died, Lynn was convinced we should travel to her bedside. I phoned the hospital, to be told there was no need to visit, as mum's life was not in any danger. However, Lynn was insistent we visit that night, and I knew that I had to be guided by her. So, after a gruelling day at work, we set off in appalling driving conditions to visit my mother, one hundred miles away. When we arrived, my mother was attached to a morphine syringe driver; she was unconscious, and almost unrecognisable. She was as white as the sheets and seemed so frail, dwarfed by the hospital bed. Her breathing was erratic and laboured. I could not bear to see mum that way, so

I went outside to collect my thoughts, leaving Lynn by the bedside while I walked around the hospital grounds, to compose myself. When I returned to my mother's bedside, she was dead. I could not believe my eyes; it was so sudden. Fifteen minutes earlier, she had been alive, and now it was too late. I did not have the chance to say goodbye. I was so shocked. As we drove home, I asked Lynn to describe to me mum's last few minutes before she died. Lynn told me that she had witnessed something quite extraordinary, and believed my mother had a deathbed conversion to Christianity. I could not believe my ears. My mum had attended church for most of her life. Lynn had occasionally spoken to her about having a relationship with Jesus but, like me, mum thought it was all a bit emotional and unnecessary. Mum would occasionally complain to me that Lynn had sent her a little booklet about being born again, or a card or poem encouraging her to ask Jesus into her life; but we had never had a serious conversation about her faith.

As we drove home, Lynn told me what had happened. Apparently, Lynn had asked God not to let mum die until she had put her life right with him and was guaranteed a place in heaven. She had felt God tell her to go to the hospital and pray with Mary. When we arrived at the hospital, the room was crowded with people but, having found herself alone with mum, she knew that it was her time to talk to her. As she held mum's hand, she stroked her hair and asked Jesus to give her his wisdom, and the words to speak to her. She also asked him to set an angel on the corridor, to give them peace and quiet together. Even though mum was unable to be roused, Lynn knew from her nurse training that the last of the senses to fade is hearing, and she knew mum could hear her. She asked her if she could remember all the times she had spoken to her about Jesus. She explained that she was very close to leaving her life on earth, and not to be frightened. Lynn told her that she would hold her hand this side of life, and that Jesus would take hold of her hand on the other side of life. There was nothing to fear because, between them, they would always hold on to her. All she had to do was to ask

Jesus into her heart, and say sorry for all the things she had said and done to offend him. It did not matter if she could not say the words aloud; she could speak them in her mind. Jesus would hear her prayer and honour her commitment by taking her hand and leading her into heaven. Mum had lain motionless, her breathing heavy and noisy; and again Lynn urged her to say the prayer in her heart. She also told her she had been a good mother and it was time to let go and go and party with Jesus. All she had to do was say the prayer in her heart; look for Jesus; take his hand, and go with him into heaven —with our love. A few moments later, mum sat bolt upright in bed. She did not open her eyes but moved her head slowly, several times, from left to right —as if scanning the room. Suddenly, she sat still, gave a huge smile, lay back down against the pillows, and died. Her noisy breathing simply stopped. Lynn said it was all so sudden that she was stunned. She was not the only one!

For weeks, I could not stop thinking about mum's death, and kept asking Lynn to go over the events, again and again. Each time, her story was the same. Mum had sat up, looked around, smiled, and died. Lynn was unshakable in her belief that my mother had met with Jesus and died peacefully.

During the next few months, I became aware of just how strong Lynn's faith was. We started to discuss events in our lives, and she described how she had prayed for us throughout our marriage. Her answers to prayer amazed me. I started to believe that things just could not have happened by coincidence. In March, we held a memorial service for my mother. I was unable to say anything, as it was so upsetting for me. However, Lynn was our family representative. Her words touched my heart, and I recognised something very special in my wife. I started to search for more answers. During the following months, I continued to read the Bible and realised that I did now believe in God. I discussed this with Lynn, who asked me if I believed Jesus was the Son of God. At that time, I did not; I still had more research to do, to answer that question.

Out of the blue, our youngest child, Laura, asked why she

had not been baptised as a baby, as her brother had been. I told her that we were too busy, and it was sort of forgotten. Lynn told her that it was because I was so anti-Christian. I was taken aback, as I had no recollection of this. Laura announced that she wanted to be baptised in our village church. I agreed to support her in this, and Lynn contacted the local vicar. Ivan Butcher came to visit us and was very clear about what baptism meant. He was not prepared to baptise Laura unless we all realised the importance of the vows we were taking. I was forced to study the vows, part of which included a declaration that I believed in God the Father, Jesus, and the Holy Spirit; and renounced the devil. Ivan was uncompromising: I had to understand what I was saying before God. This was 'Advanced level' stuff for me. During the baptism preparation, Ivan and I became friends. He was such an uncomplicated man; I enjoyed our intelligent discussions, and respected his faith in God. We planned that Laura would be baptised in the summer.

April 17th, 2000, started like any other day. I had been to work, arriving home tired but eager to talk to Lynn about God. We snuggled down in front of the fire. Both our teenage children went to bed unusually early, and our home was quiet and peaceful. We talked for hours about God. Eventually, Lynn asked me, "Robert, do you believe in God?"

"Yes," I replied.

She then asked, "Do you believe that Jesus is the Son of God?"

"Yes, I do," I said.

Lynn was quiet for a few moments and then asked me if I believed Jesus rose from the dead. I told her that I did. The atmosphere was electric. Lynn now looked at me and said, "Well Rob, you have a choice to make: do you want to ask Jesus into your life?" I was not sure what I would have to do, so Lynn explained I would simply have to say a prayer, and that was it. I asked her to run through the prayer before I said it. The next thing I knew was that we were both kneeling on the floor in front of the fire and I was asking Jesus to come into my life and forgive me for my past. Lynn laughed and cried at the same time. She was so excited that, in spite of the fact that it was, by now, one o'clock in the morning, she reached for the phone and called her friend, Micki, to share the good news.

We went to church together the following Sunday, and told Ivan what had happened. I cannot say that I felt different after asking Jesus into my life, except that I felt absolutely at peace with myself.

Two weeks later, we found ourselves in a time of crisis. Lynn was suddenly taken seriously ill. She developed peritonitis, caused by a perforated gangrenous appendix. I knew that my wife's life was in danger, and I knew now that God could heal her. I found myself continuously calling on God for his protection on Lynn's life. Overnight, my dependence on him became total. Lynn came home from hospital two weeks later, still very ill and in need of nursing. Two weeks later, I was racked with back pain, and could not walk. It was so bad that, for the first time in my life, I took time off work. Lynn and I were like helpless infants. The following week we somehow managed to get to church. We were both very fragile, and I could barely get out of the car. The pain was so bad that I still could not walk unaided. We were a sorry pair! I asked Jesus to heal me, as we really could not manage as we were. During the service, I felt the presence of the Lord. By the time I returned to the car, I was pain-free, fully mobile —and completely healed. I knew that I had received a supernatural healing from Jesus.

My spiritual hunger increased, and we decided to attend an Alpha course together. I read Nicky Gumbel's book *Questions of Life* several times and a book by Merlin Carothers, entitled *Power in Praise*. My spiritual life was transformed. At Christmas we were both confirmed in our parish church. It was a wonderful occasion, and very special for me as I was at long last making a public declaration that I now knew Jesus.

When I look back at my life as a non-Christian, I can hardly remember the times I gave Lynn a hard time for her faith. It seems now to be as though I were another person then. I am so sorry for her, and all the other Christians to whom I was so appallingly rude. I am so grateful she stood by me and invested all those years of prayer in me, and I look forward to spending the rest of our lives together, as God intended, as a Christian couple.

I feel like the prodigal son. Now that I have a relationship with Jesus, I can see how, even though I rejected him, he never gave up on me. Through Lynn, he provided for all our needs. I am amazed by the answers to prayer, which we have received over the years. My life is totally transformed. I am in a good general practice, live in a beautiful part of the country, and have stopped fighting Jesus. I am far more relaxed now, and certainly more cheerful about things. I pray a lot, and ask God, time and time again, to give me his help and energy to cope with various situations in my work and family life. The biggest difference is that I worry much less. The more I pray, read the Bible, and commune with God, the greater is my awareness of the work of the Holy Spirit within. I spend at least two hours a day in the car, driving to and from work, and this gives me a lot of praying time. I read the Bible daily, usually during my lunch break, and this makes a huge difference to my day.

I am hugely blessed to do a job where I can help people. I can see so clearly that many who walk into my surgery are in emotional pain because they do not have the Lord in their lives. They stumble from one relationship to another, collecting hurts, and then wonder why they are depressed. It is such a tragedy. My ability to do the 'right thing' becomes easier. I now find bad language offensive, and cannot stand gossip. I find myself dampening down rude conversations or suggestive remarks, whereas before I just accepted that this was the way people behaved. Now I feel that I can put a stop to these things without too much fuss. I am becoming increasingly confident about dealing with unexpected requests and problems. I can look someone in the eye and say, "I don't think that's a good idea", or, "I don't think you should do that." I have a new-found moral confidence.

My attitude towards Lynn, fellow Christians, and Jesus, is

completely different. Lynn and I are much closer; our relationship feels complete and fulfilled. We are, at last, a partnership, in every area of our relationship.

These verses, in Paul's letter to the Philippians, sum up my life perfectly:

I have known what it is to be in need and I have known what it is to have plenty. I have learnt the secret of being content in any and every situation, whether well fed or hungry, whether living in plenty or in want. I can do everything through him that gives me strength.

Philippians 4:12–14

My one regret is that we did not bring up the children together in a Christian home, though I am confident that Lynn has put in all the groundwork. Both children are still in shock about my conversion. Neither of them is interested in Christianity at the moment, but I know God will turn them around one day. I look forward to the day that we can worship the Lord together with our two children. I know it will happen, because God answers all our prayers. It took me nearly thirty years to learn that lesson. For now, it is time to concentrate our prayers on our children. It is the least I can do. I have certainly made a lot of mistakes in my life, and I do sometimes wonder whether I might not have made so many had I become a Christian sooner!

If I were to offer advice to anyone wrestling with God, it would have to be in two parts. The first is to Christian wives. I cannot encourage you enough to behave in a Christian manner, and stick to God's rules. Set a good example in your home. Do not get angry with your husband's unbelief; be patient, and teach by example, no matter how hard this is. My second piece of advice is to the non-Christian husband. First and foremost, well done for getting this far: reading this book is a huge step. My advice to you is to read the Gospels a couple of times, and then make your decision. It does not take very long to work through Matthew, Mark, Luke and

John. Keep an open heart as you read. Try the simple prayer which I prayed; then try and tell me you do not believe!

If you try to work things out intellectually, you will never cross the divide. The Word of God says he has revealed the truth to the simple and concealed it from the wise. This always struck me as an 'upside down' verse, but I soon discovered its truth. I tried to work things out through my own intellect. Having submitted to Jesus, he has shown me the truth. Jesus said, **"I praise you, Father, Lord of heaven and earth, because you have hidden these things from the wise and learned, and revealed them to little children."**[1]

At last, Jesus makes sense to me, and he did not need to use my intellect to teach me. He just needs us to be willing to listen. That small prayer — "God I don't believe in you, but if you are there, show me" — revolutionised my life. I thank God for his patience, and for blessing me with a praying wife.

[1] See Matt. 11:25

2

Lynn Forrester

Every time I attend church with my husband Robert, I pinch myself and give thanks to God for working a miracle in our lives. When we have Christian friends around for a meal, and Rob is enthusing about Jesus, or the two of us are discussing Scripture, I could faint with pleasure. It is such a contrast to the first eighteen years of our marriage. My husband was a devout atheist; and if Jesus could melt my husband's heart, he can melt anyone's. No one is too hard a nut to crack for the Lord.

I often ask myself whether this is the same man who stopped me from taking the children to church; the same man who would become enraged if I left my Bible or Christian books around the house; the same man who often persecuted me in my own home.

For eighteen years I had lived with a man who would either attack me verbally or lapse into a dark mood when I mentioned Jesus. At the slightest whiff of how I felt about the Lord, Rob's face would go bright red, a little muscle on his left cheek bone would twitch and he would become tight lipped. I could almost visualise two little horns popping up on top of his head. He only needed a pitchfork and long red tail to complete the picture and we were in action. I knew the second the twitching started that I was in for a rough ride.

In fairness to Rob, I was the one that had changed, not him. He had married a normal girl, and by his second wedding anniversary was married to a religious nut!

I did not want to be a Christian; I was terrified of being labelled a weak freak. I put up a sterling fight for months, but knew, in the end, I had to make a choice. Having realised that Jesus was who he said he was, I couldn't ignore him.

It would be fair to call myself a reluctant Christian; I certainly struggled with the concept of asking Jesus into my life. What an idiot I was. Throughout my Christian life, the only person who tore my heart to shreds was the one person I least expected it from—my husband, Robert. There is no doubt about it, being a Christian was a two-edged sword. Because of my faith I had huge hassle from my husband, but I know that had I not had Jesus in my life, we would not be together now.

Initially, I would plot all sorts of *chance* meetings with Christian friends, in the hope that Rob would warm to them and, ultimately, Jesus. It never worked. When I took Rob to a FGBMFI dinner, the military planning was befitting any presidential head of state! Timing, seating, conversation were all well rehearsed. It took weeks of plotting. We even engineered who to keep him away from. The known 'Bible bashers' were intercepted by a highly trained team of friends, to steer them off course and divert their attention elsewhere. We even planned the menu to include Rob's favourite foods.

Needless to say, it was all an unmitigated disaster. Rob is not a violent man, but I think I came the closest I have ever been to being throttled that night! He was vile; I was disappointed; and my friends were exhausted by weeks of combat training. Everybody had a lousy evening. I decided to leave Rob to God—until the next time.

I would often get fed up with waiting for God to act, and could not resist giving a little help now and again. I used to tell myself that God was obviously tied up with something else, or had 'gone away on holiday', so it was up to me to give

Rob a bit of a nudge. God always seemed so painfully slow. I knew he could zap Rob in an instant, and, when I get to heaven, I look forward to asking him why he did not do so. Somehow, I have a sinking feeling it was more to do with me changing than Rob.

When the children were little, Rob escaped to the pub every Saturday night. He would set off with our golden Labrador, and walk a ten mile round trip to the pub. I used to joke with him that he would meet an angel on the way back, and then he would believe in Jesus. I cannot remember where I got that idea from, but I said it as regularly as clockwork. He never did get his angelic visitation, though I am sure God did send his angels to bring him home. Something must have held him up!

Before we had the children we had far more freedom as a couple and did more together. Our main pastime was partying, but when the children came along I soon lost my desire to party. I was always so busy and tired and, besides, I did not want to get hammered all the time. I grew out of it much more quickly than Rob. I can see now that Rob thought it was because I had become a Christian that I did not want to go out with him, which was not the case at all. Unwittingly, I reinforced his opinion that religion was about what you could not do, rather than what you can do.

I tried so hard to get Rob to see that there was a huge difference between religion and a personal relationship with God, but got nowhere. I used to engineer 'chance' meetings with friends, hoping that once Rob got to know Christians he would see Jesus in them. It was fruitless really; it took me a long time to work out that we are born again in God's timing, not ours. My efforts only served to irritate him and drive him further away from God. Because Rob is a doctor, I thought that if he could see a healing miracle then he would become a believer, so I started to look around for suitable healing services to which I could take him. At the time there were stories of people being healed from painful hip disorders, commonly caused by one leg being longer than the other. I longed to see a miracle at one of these meetings, so that I could impress Rob and take him along; but I wanted to make sure it was genuine. I remember my friend and myself measuring each other's legs before we went into the service, just to make sure no one could pretend we had been miraculously cured. We used to have some laughs planning Rob's conversion, but there were plenty of sad times too.

Throughout the children's early years, I always drew Jesus into their lives. When they were poorly or upset, we always prayed together, quietly and sensitively. The children accepted that Rob did not like Jesus and was not his friend yet. They would sometimes ask Rob about Jesus, but they soon learned it was a 'no go' area. From a tender age they knew how to please daddy, and talking Jesus was bound to evoke a negative response. I prayed with the children in secret. Providentially, Robert was rarely home at the children's bedtimes, and was not privy to our prayers. I believe that solid foundations were laid for my children during those times. Eventually, Rob told me he was unhappy with the children's religious indoctrination, and he wanted us to stop going to church. This caused me great anguish, and I called out to God for his intervention. I coped with not being able to talk to the children about Jesus by praying for them when they were asleep. I would pray the Lord's blessings on them, whispering that Jesus loved them. I desperately wanted God to change Rob's heart. Instead, he chose to change mine.

Being in church with two children with no support was really difficult. At that time we did not have a church crèche, so I and a couple of other mums would sit in the vestry, straining to hear the service, whilst trying to keep our children quiet. The church family were oblivious to our difficulties and, on one occasion, someone asked me to leave the church because my child was being too noisy. She subsequently apologised, but the incident underlined the point that attending church was a real battle for me.

I started to go to church on my own, but leaving the children with Rob was more trouble than it was worth. Rob was so moody when I returned home from church, that I decided it was right to stay at home and minister to my family.

I continued to worship the Lord, and the only place I could do that in absolute freedom was in my car. My little 2CV became a mobile church. I would have Christian music blaring and praised God to my heart's content. I devoured teaching tapes and was 'self-churched' for a long time. When I could, I met with Christian friends for prayer and support. Not all Christians were as on the ball as I would have hoped. There were times when I felt really worn down by the struggle of living with a non-Christian. I usually kept a brave face on things, because I did not want to be disloyal to Rob. He is a good man and my best friend. He was really only painful when Jesus hit him head on. I could not bear the thought of people thinking badly of him, so I generally kept things to myself. I think now that was a huge mistake; there was a spiritual battle going on for my husband, and people should have been praying into the situation. Anyhow, on one occasion I was at a ladies' Bible group and I broke down in tears. I remember feeling as though my heart was breaking, and Christian friends gathered around, laid hands on me, and started praying. It was an amazing feeling, being so loved and prayed for. During the prayers, one woman said to me, "Lynn, the Lord will bless you because you are crying with your head bent." I was so shocked; I could not believe she had said such a stupid thing. How do people normally cry? —head held high; 'come look at me'? I am sorry to say that, in an instant, I decided never to open up again in the group. From then on, I struggled on alone.

Because I attended church on my own, I felt incomplete. There were so many things I missed out on that I felt like a second class citizen. I was unable to participate fully in church life: since I could not attend regularly, serve within the church, or tithe, one always felt like an outsider.

My loyalties were constantly divided. I longed to serve Jesus and to be in the company of Christians. I made the mistake of really believing that unless I was in church I was not serving the Lord. It took me a long time to realise that I had been placed in one of the hardest mission fields in the world: my own home. I was doing the Lord's work; I was ministering to my husband and children every day of my life. I completely underestimated the role God had given me. I longed for my children to be influenced by wonderful, godly men and women, but it was not to be at that time. The Lord gave me a verse, "I will restore to you the years that the locusts have eaten." Well, he is certainly doing that. Nowadays, listening to Rob pray and praise the Lord wipes out all the years of loneliness and disappointment.

Over the years, I stopped plotting and learnt to put my energy into *praying* for Rob. Without realising it, I was the one who started to change. I accepted that Rob would only come to the Lord in God's time, not mine. That was disappointing, but it took me a long while to realise that I was not the boss here. As a family, we missed out on a lot of social events as Rob would sit miserably and not engage in conversation with anyone. It was so painful for me to watch, as Rob is one of the funniest men I have ever met. He has a sharp wit and is very entertaining. I always felt as though I had a truculent teenager in tow, and would be apologetic and embarrassed by his behaviour. We would always row about his conduct, once we were home. So, to keep the peace, we stopped accepting invitations from Christians. For their part, they got fed up with having 'Mr Misery' spoiling their events, and I cannot say I blamed them.

A great turning point for me was realising that I was not responsible for Rob's behaviour —he was. Having accepted that, I felt more relaxed around him and our friends. I stopped making excuses for him and started being honest. I would tell people he was anti-Christian and did not want to be in their company, and they graciously accepted that.

Being unable to attend church was difficult for me, and served to increase my sense of isolation and separation from both the church family and my husband. Rob asked me to stop going to church on many occasions, but what he was really asking me to do was to stop loving Jesus. I told him I could give up church, but not loving the Lord—and I never did.

Because we lived in a small island, Rob was determined

that our two children would go to boarding school in England when they were thirteen years old. I was vehemently opposed to this, and we argued endlessly about their future. We talked about it for hours. Rob would not budge, and was determined they would leave Jersey in order to broaden their education. In the end, I finally caught on, and fell on my knees before God. I remember it as if it were yesterday. I knelt beside our bed in floods of tears, absolutely heartbroken at the thought of not steering my children through their teen years. I was bereft and grieving. I called out to God and asked him to stop Rob from taking my children away from me. I asked God to take every penny we had, to stop Rob's plans. I stopped arguing with Rob and left God on the case. Ten years later, I was to learn that prayers should come with a health warning: **"If you don't mean, it don't ask."** The year before Edward was due to start boarding school, we lost every penny we had. But I kept my children at home as requested—not a bad swap!

Looking back, I can see that I did not handle Rob too well, and made lots of mistakes in the early days. Because I had been completely un-churched before my own conversion, I had had no idea there was such prejudice towards Christians. Once I had asked Jesus into my reluctant heart, I was propelled into an amazing frenzy of discovery. I could not contain the miracle of what had happened to me. I could not understand why Jesus was such a big secret. Nor could I understand why Rob was so reluctant to share this wonderful part of my life. If only I had been given wise counsel from within the church, I think I could have saved myself a lot of heartache and eased Rob into the reality of what was happening to me. It took me a long time to apply Philippians 4:4–8 to my life: to rejoice, not be anxious, and to pray with thanksgiving.

Before becoming a Christian, I had explored other religions from an intellectual perspective. I was interested in Buddhism, and read a lot of books written by a Tibetan high lama. I found the teachings sincere—until I found out that my Tibetan high lama was actually a plumber from Devon:

somehow the attraction wore off. Like many young people, I dabbled with spiritualism, making the grave mistake of thinking of it as 'entertainment'. I did not take any of it seriously; it seemed harmless then, before I knew of its dangers. But now that my eyes had been opened spiritually, I could see clearly false religions for what they are, and knew in my spirit, personally, that Jesus was for real, and that I was a temple of the Holy Spirit. No matter how I tried, of course, I could not get Rob to see things as I did.

Life was so difficult for me; I loved Rob so much, and I loved the Lord. Rob seemed unable to co-exist peacefully with my faith. I enjoyed my husband's company, and we agreed on so many issues, yet the most fundamental difference existed between us. We just could not agree about the existence of God. Rob was usually such a placid, gentle man; the only thing that provoked a hostile response from him was Christianity. We had only been married eighteen months when I became a Christian, and I did not have the maturity or confidence in our marriage to know how to handle him. Without realising it, every time I declared my faith I drove an even greater wedge between us. I felt passionately that I could not pretend with Rob: he was my best friend, and I had to be totally honest with him. I still stand by that, but perhaps I could have been a little more sensitive towards his needs. There were times that I was really angry with him for not believing, and I let it show.

Eventually, after a long time, I learnt that my only proper course of action was to pray for him to know the love of Jesus in his life and be born again. I prayed for eighteen years, and not once during that time did I doubt that God would answer my prayer. There were times when I despaired, and felt I could not go on any longer. But, I always knew that, one day, God would bring Rob to his knees, just as God's word promised.

During our marriage we have been through a lot of trials. We have moved home eleven times in as many years, suffered bereavements, near-bankruptcy, unemployment and hardship. No matter how bad things were, Rob still would not have anything to do with God. With every new trial we faced, I always thought that was going to be the time that Rob would ask the Lord into his heart. I expected Rob to call out to Jesus in desperation, but he never did. He felt that, as head of the family, he was the one to sort things out. As far as Rob was concerned, praying was like talking to the fairies at the bottom of the garden. The truth was, we did not face one crisis without Jesus. I called on God throughout our marriage, and he always answered in amazing ways.

Throughout the years of waiting for Rob, God built up my faith. Instead of dissolving into a 'pity party', I decided to become as strong a Christian as I could. I had no doubt that God is faithful to his word. When I die, if they cut me open they will find the following verse running through my body, like a stick of Blackpool rock, **"Believe in the Lord Jesus, and you will be saved —you and your household."** (Acts 16:31). I knew it was only a matter of time. It was really hard to stand on that promise sometimes, especially when Rob was being so vile about my faith; but I hung on to it.

Rob is such an intelligent man; he always seemed to have the right words to argue that God did not exist. I did not have the words or knowledge to fight back effectively —or so I thought! Often, our discussion about God would leave me feeling worn out and inadequate. But my commitment to pray for Rob was constantly renewed. When he was not wiping the floor with me intellectually, his behaviour would handicap me. He was often moody, verbally aggressive and insulting towards God and the people with whom I mixed. Eventually, I learnt to stop reacting to *his* behaviour and to change *mine*.

Through the years, the Lord brought some wonderful people into my life, many of them women in the same position as myself. We would encourage each other and regularly prayed together for our families. We did not always meet for formal prayer, but simply made the most of every opportunity we had. It could be a chance meeting in a car park; over coffee; or whilst walking on the beach. If we felt burdened for our husbands, we prayed. God faithfully answered our prayers. The following extract is taken from a diary entry, dated June 1996.

> It is now sixteen years since my conversion to Christianity. I am now older and wiser and, thanks to God's infinite patience, I am becoming the wife God wants me to be. One of my main roles in our family is to intercede for my husband and children. Not on a superficial "please save them" level, but on a deep spiritual level that only Jesus through the power of his Holy Spirit can reveal to me. This has meant learning deeper things of God—things I would much rather leave to someone else. Thankfully, God is a patient teacher. I have absolute faith that my husband will be born again. Being a devout atheist is no problem to my God. Nor is the fact that my husband only uses the name of God to curse. Robert Forrester belongs to Jesus. Nothing will separate me from that assurance. Scripture says, **"Believe in the Lord Jesus, and you will be saved —you and your household."** Well, I'm holding out for that because I know God is faithful; it will happen one day. *Acts 16:31* Thank you, Father.

I only had to wait three more years for God to change my husband's heart and answer my prayers. I started to look back at Rob's life and asked the Holy Spirit to show me any areas that were blocking Rob's walk with the Lord. A week later, Rob's mother showed me some old family photographs, amongst which were snaps of her brother in full freemason's regalia. She proudly informed us he had been a 'grand master'. I was amazed that she had never mentioned this before, and I knew it was the Lord at work. I started praying immediately, asking the Lord to free Rob from any effects of family involvement in freemasonry.

We moved back to England in 1994, after God answered my prayer to take all our money from us to stop our children going to boarding school! We were in low spirits: the wrench was enormous and I thought my heart would break. I can honestly say it was the lowest point in my life. I felt that I did not have the energy to relocate and make new friends. We had lost everything financially and I felt battered. But I had prayed about the move and knew God had a plan for us. I never lost faith that he knew what he was doing, even if I did not know! One verse that bought me immense comfort was, **"A bruised reed he will not break, and a smouldering wick he will not snuff out"** (Isaiah 42:3). That described my condition perfectly. I was a bruised reed, and I was concerned that I would break. The Lord soon honoured my faithfulness. I decided that it was time to make a stand for Jesus and start attending church again. I just knew that I had to get serious with God, as my faith was so battered. I knew I needed to be in fellowship, as I was in such a painful and dark phase of life. I believe that a major turning point in both my life and Rob's was when I started meeting with a group of women to pray for our non-Christian husbands. Not only did we encourage each other through prayer and friendship, but also we entered into a real battle for our men. The Bible tells us that we wrestle not against flesh and blood, but against powers, principalities, rulers and authorities. So we stepped out in faith and learnt how to intercede for our husbands. Over the years, one by one, our husbands came to know the Lord. At times it was hard waiting for 'Rob's turn', but I became more determined to stay positive —and to keep on praying. I know that was as a direct answer to prayer.

God saw my aching heart for my children's spiritual needs, too, and he honoured me. I desperately longed for them to attend a Christian school —and they did. Their head master, Christopher Bacon, was an honourable, godly man, and he made a huge impression on Rob. Thanks to that wonderful man of God, our children were able to receive an excellent education in a Christian environment. At last, our children were fed the word of God. I felt that the Lord honoured my faithfulness by restoring to me the years that the locusts had eaten. Both our children asked the Lord into their lives whilst in the junior school.

This became my prayer and source of encouragement:

I lift my eyes to the hills—
where does my help come from?
My help comes from the LORD,
the Maker of heaven and earth.

Psalm 121:1–2

A year later, just as we were getting back on our feet, we went through another major financial crisis, and things were really bad for us. I toyed with the idea of changing our name to 'Job'! However, Jesus was there with me all the time.

On one sharp, crisp day, Rob and I went for a walk on the hillside above our home. Rob dropped the bombshell: we were to face another huge financial blow. I could not believe it, and remember saying to God, "Not again, Lord, not again." As we walked down the hill, hand in hand, I noticed our shadows bouncing ahead of us. It looked as if there were three people walking down the hill. A peace came over me, and I knew the Lord was telling me, "I am with you, Lynn, don't be frightened." I knew immediately that God was in the situation. Once again, I told Rob that I would pray about it, and he once again gave me a weak, patronising smile; the smile that said, 'Really, Lynn, isn't it about time you stopped believing all this rubbish?' Suddenly, it was as though a light switched on in my head. I realised that a familiar behaviour pattern seemed to be emerging. We would have a crisis, I would pray like fury, God would intervene, and Rob thought the crisis was resolved because of his own efforts. I looked at Rob, realising it was time to let go, and let God have his way with him. We had been through so much, and God had always brought us through. It was time to trust God for Rob. I explained to Rob that I understood how he felt towards God, but asked if he would say one prayer and then I would never ask him to pray again —ever. To my amazement he said 'yes'; I know now that it was simply to 'shut me up', but those few simple words opened the floodgates to God's faithfulness toward Rob:

"God, I don't believe in you; but if you are there, please show me...."

I fully expected a bolt of lightning to come down from heaven and zap Rob right there and then —I was so disappointed when it did not! Little did I know that God would start the process straight away, but in his way, not mine.

I was quite slow reading the signs that Rob was thawing. It was probably because I had plotted and planned so many times to no avail that I had become content, accepting that everything was in God's hands, not mine. I had no idea Rob was secretly reading the Bible, listening to choral evensong or collecting Christian freebies from *The Daily Telegraph*.

During Rob's mum's illness, I noticed a huge softening of his attitude towards my faith. I felt able to tell him I was praying for his mother; and I did not receive the usual aggressive response. He was just very quiet; I assumed he could not be bothered to harangue me. God was quietly and gently at work behind the scenes, and I had no idea.

I considered it a huge privilege to have shared my mother-in-law's deathbed conversion. I was very nervous about telling Rob, but I knew I just had to tell him, whatever the fallout; little realising that God had already done the groundwork, and that the night would prove to be a dramatic turning point in Rob's life. Interestingly, after her death, I found a neat little pile of all the cards and tracts I had sent my mother-in-law over the years. I felt that this was the Lord's confirmation that, even though Mary was disgruntled with my efforts to convert her, she had taken notice.

During the following year, Rob would often ask me to run through the night's events again; clearly, he was moved, and he asked me many questions. "What made you think we had to go and visit that night?" "Why were you so sure?" "Why did you pray with Mary?" My answer was always the same: "It was the Holy Spirit directing me; we were meant to be with her when she died."

Rob started asking me questions about Jesus and my faith, often going over the same ground again. I answered as honestly as I could, and felt relaxed talking to him. This was a new thing for us. It became routine: every time we sat down together, he would ask me another question about God.

We spent hours discussing the difference between religion and personal faith. I think I probably went into 'prayer over-drive' around that time. I was happy to discuss my faith with Rob, and relieved that the animosity towards God had eased off. I still had no idea what was about to happen.

The night Rob gave his life to the Lord will remain etched in my mind forever; it was amazing. I wanted to tell the whole world. In fact I did, in a small way. Apart from waking up my friend at one o'clock in the morning, I posted an announcement on a Christian internet site! The web response was amazing. This is an excerpt from my diary, dated 19th April 2000:

> Something wonderful has happened—Rob is born again!!! We knelt together on the sitting room carpet, in front of the dying fire, and said the prayer of commitment together. The very thing I had dreamed of so many times, in so many ways, happened in the most unexpected way.
>
> I led my husband to the Lord. I can't believe it!!! The atmosphere was electric and I wept like a baby. Such indescribable joy is impossible to put into words....
>
> I just want to praise Jesus; I can't stop singing worship songs. Thank you, Heavenly Father, for answering my prayers for Rob. Bless you, Father.

The joy I felt that night, and every day since Rob became a Christian, is so real. I cannot describe how wonderful it is for Rob and I to be at one about Jesus: it is truly amazing. At last, I feel as if we are completely at peace with each other. I do not know whether or why God wanted Rob to wait all these years until he put his life right with Jesus, but I know that things happen in the Lord's perfect timing, not mine.

Because we have such different personalities, I knew Rob would want to attend a traditional, Church of England service. I prefer more relaxed, charismatic services, but I was so happy to be in church with my husband that I did not mind where we went. We attended an Alpha course together, and were confirmed together at Christmas. Friends who had joined me in prayer for Rob came and supported us. It was a very special day. We are now in a much bigger church, which is 'on fire' for Jesus, and I cannot wait to see what plans the Lord has for us as a couple.

However, I know that, for many people, the time of waiting is not over yet. If that applies to you, then I want to encourage you, right now, to take on board the fact that Jesus loves you just as much as he loves me; and that your time for rejoicing will come. That is God's promise to you. Pray for your partner, and never give up believing that, one day, your heart will sing when Jesus honours your prayers. Do not be discouraged when you see everyone else's husband but yours coming to the Lord. Be patient, and trust that Jesus knows the right time for you both. Refuse to buy into the lie that God has forgotten you.

"Be strong and courageous. Do not be afraid or terrified of them, for the LORD your God goes with you; he will never leave you nor forsake you."

Deuteronomy 31:6

Stay close to Jesus. Try to get as much fellowship as you can, and build yourself up in the Lord. Listen to Christian radio and television, use audio cassettes to be taught and nourished with the word of God, but be sensitive. Pray without ceasing. Get your friends to pray, get strangers to pray, take advantage of every available prayer opportunity you can; love your husband to bits, and be the best wife you can be. It is my prayer and heart's desire that God will bless and encourage you every time you pick up this book; that he will teach you through his loving Holy Spirit how to pray and claim all that is rightfully yours; and especially for the salvation of those held nearest to your heart.

I pray that the God of grace, our Jehovah Jireh, will bless and keep you in your journey, as he did me.

3

Mike Tindall

I had an exceptionally happy childhood, and was blessed with wonderful parents and grandparents. I knew total love and security at home, and was always made to feel special. Because of my football skills, I had a high profile at school and was popular with my teachers and peers. Looking back, I realise I was a bit of a 'golden boy'. My father frequently told me I was the best, and I never doubted him.

Although religion was never mentioned in our house, my father had a respect for Christian ethics, and he would never let me play football on a Sunday, always maintaining that it was a special day. I would beg him to let me join the other lads in the park, but he never gave in. When our first child was born, my father said that we should go to church and give thanks to God, because our son was perfect —extraordinary, as he was not himself a Christian.

I left school at fifteen years of age and went straight to Aston Villa Football Club as a junior team player. Three years later, I was playing in the first team. Such rapid promotion was unheard of in those days; players were usually well into their twenties before being selected to play for the first team. Football opened the door to a privileged life for me—

a lifestyle that most people could only dream about. It was wonderful: I was playing football, keeping fit, and getting paid three times the average man's wage, all by the time I was eighteen years old. As a celebrity, I enjoyed the best that life could offer. Footballers were public heroes; ordinary men and women 'idol worshipped' us. I never had to queue for anything; shopkeepers would not charge me, clubs and pubs were the same. I was earning a huge amount of money, and did not have to spend it, as people wanted to show their appreciation by giving me things. I had a high public and media profile, simply because I could play football. On ten occasions, I played for the England under 23 team. Sharing the pitch with great players—like Bobby Moore, George Best, Bobby Charlton and Jimmy Greaves—was a great honour. I loved not only the game but also the lifestyle that came with it. The only negative thing I had to cope with was heckling from the terraces: the fans would soon let us know if we were not playing well; but I developed a 'thick skin'.

It is fair to say that I was a bit of a ladies' man. I dated beautiful women, and had a bit of a reputation, but always knew that, when I met the right girl, I would not be carrying on with the single lifestyle, unlike many of my peers. I met Thora when I was twenty one, first noticing her because she never stopped talking! We married in a haze of publicity, then settled into a glamorous lifestyle. Unlike today's top players, I was not paid thousands of pounds per game, but we certainly enjoyed a good life, and wanted for nothing. I had found the love of my life, and was happy to share all I had with her.

Several years later, things changed for me, following an accident during a football match against Tottenham. I broke my leg badly, and it took me nine months to recover from my injuries. During the next four years, I had intermittent problems, and my game was never the same again. So, after fourteen years of playing for Aston Villa, I decided to transfer. At that time we had established business interests, and I was keen to stay in the Midlands, so I transferred from Aston Villa to Walsall. By my thirtieth birthday, though, I had given up professional football and was working for a non-league team part-time, whilst I concentrated on various business ventures.

Perhaps I should not have retired from the game so early, but it is easy to be wise after the event. I subsequently worked for the Vice President of Aston Villa, as his 'right hand man'. I would attend high profile events with him and, once again, I was propelled into a privileged and glamorous world, which continually took me away from home. Thora was, in effect, a single parent. This took its toll on our marriage and Thora's health.

My life had not changed much, but Thora's had. She was at home with three pre-school children, whilst I spent a lot of time on my own. She would tell me how difficult she found life, coping with a young family, but her pleas fell on deaf ears for a long time. The strain eventually caught up with us and, after five years, I left my job. Thora's health deteriorated further, and she had a breakdown. We had a succession of business enterprises, and eventually left Birmingham for Bournemouth. It was a beautiful town, affluent and peaceful, and I felt we could be happy there.

We bought a greengrocery business, which very quickly became a huge success, so we decided to buy another shop. The second shop was bigger and more adventurous and, once again, we enjoyed a high standard of living. We ate out regularly, wore designer clothes, and lived in a beautiful house. Thora seemed much happier with our new life, but there was one 'fly in the ointment': an extremely kind, caring member of a local Baptist church, whose name was Dorothy. She tried to persuade Thora to attend church with her. Many of our customers attended a small church close to our shop, and they would often try to talk to us about Jesus. To add insult to injury, a Baptist minister moved into the house opposite ours, and he often extended a hand of friendship, which we declined to accept. Everywhere we turned, we were surrounded by Christians; there seemed to be one on every street corner, trying to get us to go to church! We both considered them real pests.

I thought we were set for life in Bournemouth, but I had

not anticipated the recession. Suddenly, the tourists stopped visiting, and a combination of unemployment and poor British weather emptied the town overnight. This, of course, affected our trade, and I felt it was time to get out and move into a more lucrative line of business. Recession or not, people still liked to drink alcohol, so I decided it was time to move where the money was. I started to look around the Bournemouth area for a pub to run.

During that time, my father became very ill. We had to make frequent visits back to the Midlands, to see him. Every time we returned home, there would be a gift from Dorothy waiting for us —a bunch of flowers, or a few kind words. Though we were impressed by her kindness, we still did not want anything to do with religion. However, Dorothy was relentless in her pursuit of Thora and finally, to shut her up, Thora agreed to go to church with her. Thora was not very impressed, and came home saying that they were all weird, and best avoided. We continued to ignore the local Christians until one evening, several months later, Thora attended a debate organized by a local church—to prove the existence of Jesus. It was set up as a court trial, in the town hall. People gave evidence on both sides as to the existence of Jesus Christ, and, more importantly, that he was who he said he was. I remember Thora coming home and saying that the evidence in favour of Jesus being the Son of God, and that he had been crucified, died, and rose from the dead, was huge. However, we decided that, evidence or not, it was not for us. We were far too 'normal' for all that nonsense; life was good, and we did not need God interfering in our lives.

A few weeks later, whilst I was making plans for life as a publican, Thora announced that she had become a born again Christian. I was knee deep in accountancy books at the time, and absent-mindedly replied, "Oh that's good for you. If that's your hobby, you stick with it." I had no idea what she meant, but I saw an immediate change in her.

She became a better wife in every respect. We had been in trouble for years in our marriage, and suddenly she started to behave differently towards me. Over the years, she had distanced herself from me and said, on many occasions, that she did not love me. I had never stopped loving her, and accepted that was the way our life was. We had a young family to support and, as I did not know how to meet Thora's emotional needs, my energies went into providing materially for everyone. Following Thora's surprise conversion, I noticed the immediate change in her. She was distinctly kinder, more considerate and loving; but, not wanting to encourage her 'religious mania' in any way, I did not tell her that I had noticed the change. I was busy trying to provide for my family, and I did not need this new problem. Besides, she had told me for years that she did not love me; I hardly dared believe that she could change overnight. But she did! It took me eighteen months to really believe that she loved me again. Jesus had changed her. There was no denying it: I could now see very clearly she loved me again.

Having applied to the brewery, I was soon offered a pub, but it meant leaving Bournemouth. Thora was beside herself, as she felt that being a landlady conflicted with her new-found faith. I remember vividly one night, when she sprang out of bed, ran into the sitting room and started praying. I followed her, thinking she was unwell. She told me that she could not live in a pub, because it would offend the Lord.... I said, "Well that's tough for you, and it's tough for the Lord, but that's what we are going to do." She came back to bed and, about five minutes later, she sprang out of bed again, absolutely distraught, and started pacing about the living room. Some time later, she came back to bed and announced, "It's all right. I've just had a vision about the pub; I can go." Eager for some sleep, I said, "Well done. Now get back into bed, and let's get some sleep."

Within a month, we moved to Bromsgrove. I did a two-week crash course in pub management, and I started life as a landlord. From the outset, I loved our new life; it was like a dream which had come true. The place was busy; the kids flocked in, and we made a good deal of money. There was never a dull moment as there were arguments and 'punch ups' every night. The local police spent so much time sorting out trouble in the pub that I was on first name terms with them! We had standing orders for stitches at the local hospital; yet I thought I was in heaven! I loved the buzz, and the fact that we were making a fortune. As a professional footballer, I had enjoyed the greatest lifestyle in the world. I was used to having a lot of money. I loved money, and was consumed with making still more of it. Thora had her church, and I had my pub; and I was quite happy with things the way they were—as long as she did not expect me to believe what she did.

Shortly after our move, Thora came home and announced that she had found a wonderful Baptist church locally. I encouraged her to stick with her new 'hobby', whilst I dedicated myself to the pub. It quickly consumed my life, and once again Thora was pushed out, receiving little attention from me. My life was so hectic, and the pub was all-consuming. People tend to think that being a publican is an easy life, but, on the contrary, it is a huge commitment. I was up at seven o'clock every morning. Apart from serving behind the bar, I had to organise cleaners, check and re-order stock, and supervise the draymen. The tasks were endless, and I was never able to get back upstairs to our flat until midnight every night. From the outset, Thora insisted she could not serve alcohol, and asked if she could simply serve food instead. Reluctantly, I agreed. Sadly, though, the food side of the business proved to be unprofitable, so she simply had to serve alcohol. This often proved embarrassing—for myself and the customers, as she never missed an opportunity to talk about Jesus. If she was not preaching, she was forever leaving Christian tracts and notices around the pub. She drove me mad, and I did not hide my disapproval. I could often be seen tearing up the tracts, and yelling at her to stop talking about Jesus.

After becoming a Christian, she seemed over-sensitive to everyday things. She now disliked bad language and cursing. I had always said the odd swear word, but she insisted my language was filthy. She complained about my behaviour, and hardly had a good word to say about my lifestyle,

it seemed. Despite all this, she continued to be caring, loving and attentive; and constantly told me that she loved
me. It was such a contrast to the way things had been for so
many years.

The younger customers started to bring photographs of
themselves into the pub, which soon covered a whole wall.
Week by week, these became more raunchy, and some were
almost pornographic. Thora took great offence, and begged
me to take the pictures down, but I just accused her of being
a prude. As I ignored her pleas, she apparently did the next
best thing, calling out to God to intervene. He did not let her
down, because one night the police arrived and ordered me to
remove all the photographs! Thora saw this as a huge
triumph. She told me later that the more determined I was to
keep the pictures on show, the more determined she became
in prayer. A group of Christian friends met with her regularly,
to ask God to intervene.

We rowed endlessly about her reluctance (as I saw it) to
'pull her weight' in the pub. I was sick of being dictated to by
her 'religion', and decided to sort out the issue once and for
all. I telephoned the pastor of her church, and asked to see
him. Thora begged me not to embarrass her. I went with the
intention of giving the pastor a piece of my mind. Who was
he to influence my wife? I was sick of Thora's reluctance to
serve alcohol, and her sensitivity about normal, youthful
behaviour. I felt that the church ought now to keep out of my
life. Somehow, during the meeting with Keith Blades, I lost
sight of my agenda, and he never did get my proposed 'ear
bashing'. I cannot really remember what we talked about,
but I do remember shocking myself by telling him I knew
that, one day, I would become a Christian, but at that point in
my life was not interested. I was to discover, later, that the
whole of Bromsgrove Baptist church had been praying for me
for months. Little did I know that I was no match for Jesus!

After that day, Thora's commitment to Jesus intensified.
She talked to everyone in the pub about Jesus; no one was
spared. She would serve a measure of whisky to a customer
and say, "I wish you were filled with the Holy Spirit instead

of liquid spirit." She drove me barmy. I would as good as drag her out of the bar, demanding she stop talking about religion; but she persevered, nonetheless.

She remained unhappy at having to be a landlady, but saw every customer as a God-given opportunity. Over the years, she must have spoken to hundreds of youngsters about Jesus. From my point of view, the 'last straw' was that she would round up groups of my younger customers, and take them to church: week after week. The youngsters were quite a sight, with hair of every colour: green, red, blue; all topped off with pierced body parts. Hoops, rings and chains stretching from nose to ear were a common sight. I do not know what the church people made of them, but Thora continued taking car loads of people to church for many years.

Over the years, the pub had become hugely popular, and I really thought our affluent lifestyle would last. I could not have been more wrong. Our bubble was about to burst yet again. Almost overnight, the pub emptied.

After a few months of poor trade, we were in serious financial trouble, quickly accumulating a great deal of debt. I could not believe what was happening. I was losing my business, and felt that I was losing my wife as well. She was so into her new religious life and did not seem to need me. Although Thora had told me, on numerous occasions, that Jesus had given her a greater love for me, I still felt excluded. She did everything she could to reassure me of her love and commitment, but I was not at all receptive. To make matters worse, she started to suffer from severe pre-menstrual tension (PMT). In those days, no one talked about hormones, and I did not understand what was happening to her. For half of the month she was a saint; for the rest she was a madwoman. I used these times to have a good dig at her faith, deliberately antagonising her, and never missing an opportunity to remind her that she was supposed to be a Christian and should behave in a better manner. I delighted in goading her. I recall one occasion when I had promised that we would spend the evening together. We went out for an early meal, returning home to the pub at about seven in the evening. I went down to the bar, was waylaid, then decided to make a phone call. In the meantime, Thora was upstairs, fuming that I had not kept my promise to spend time with her. Had I neglected her on a non–PMT week, I would have got a saintly response, but I hit 'hormone crisis point'. Thora tracked me down, and was furious to find me chatting on the phone, rather than spending time with her. She was so incensed at being ignored that she wrenched the phone from the wall. The whole unit was left dangling, in broken sections! To make matters worse, I carried on talking into the phone as if I were still connected. By that time, she was cross-eyed and blue in the face. When, at last, we went upstairs, into the flat, things became even worse. The fruit bowl and its contents were aimed at me! Of course, I delighted in reminding her she was supposed to show Christ in her life, not the devil. That really got her going, adding fuel to the fire.

Trade continued to go from bad to worse. No matter what I did, I could not get the customers back into the pub. I remember sitting at the table, feeling desperate about our situation, when Thora burst in and said, "The Lord has given me two fantastic words for you, Mike. He said, 'Do not worry about your life,' and, 'I am the resurrection and the life.'" She put a copy of the Bible in front of me, pointing to Matthew 6:25 and John 11:25. I read both passages, and by the time I had finished, I had steam coming out of my ears! I was enraged.

I said, "I've lost all my money. The pub is going bankrupt; and the best you can come up with is this. A guy that you can't see is telling me not to worry. It's madness!" I hurled her Bible across the room, stormed out of the house, and went to the races for the day. I did not gamble, as I had no money; I just needed to get out for a while. I returned later that evening, and sat on the edge of the bed, my head in my hands, feeling absolutely desolate.

Thora came to me, and said, "Mike, you've tried everything your way. Why don't you just give it to God?" Instead of my usual aggressive response, I suddenly had so many questions. I asked her, "If I die, will I go to heaven with you?"

She replied, "No, Mike, you'll go to hell."

No one had ever talked to me about hell before. It had never occurred to me that there was an eternal penalty for ignoring Jesus. In an instant, I remember, the fear of God gripped me; I was terrified, but I did not tell Thora. We talked for hours and, after the whole salvation message was given to me, I knew what I had to do. I kept thinking about heaven and hell, and was still gripped by fear. 'Letting go, and letting God' seemed such a huge step. I was in torment, but I knew it was my time to meet with God.

Thora led me through the sinner's prayer, and I asked Jesus into my life. I think I expected to feel something miraculous happen, but all I felt was overwhelming guilt. Suddenly, I was aware of all my faults. I was foul-mouthed, told filthy jokes, and had failed God in many ways throughout my life. I started to tell the Lord how sorry I was, for all the things I had done in my life to grieve him. I was on my knees for hours. Then I came out of the bedroom and told Thora that I did not feel any different. She simply urged me to keep praying, and reassured me that the Lord was at work. I had assumed I would feel good, having asked Jesus into my life; but I felt lousy. In the meantime, Thora was on the phone, asking all her friends to pray for me.

On the following Sunday morning, I woke up and said to Thora, "Come on, then, take me to this wonderful church of yours." She looked as if she would pass out, and encouraged me by telling me I looked like death! I went to church for the first time in my life. I sat right at the back, slumped in my seat, hoping no one would see me. Twenty minutes into the service, during the prayer time, the man sitting next to me stood up, and started talking in a foreign language. Everybody kept their heads bowed in prayer. I felt sorry for the man, who could not speak English; especially as he was evidently being ignored. What a way to treat a foreigner! After the man had finished talking, he sat down again, and there was silence in the church. I looked up at the pastor, and he started to speak. I know now that he was giving the interpretation of a 'tongue'. He spoke for some time, and I remember one particular sentence burning into the very depth of my being. He said, "Oh my son, fear not, for I am with you." Those words pierced my troubled spirit, and in an instant I met with Jesus in an amazing way.

Suddenly, I understood what the message of salvation was all about, and I knew those words were for me. In my mind's eye I saw Jesus on the cross, and I heard the Lord tell me, "My son, go and tell everyone about me." The Lord God Almighty had chosen to speak to me. I knew it was him, and I was overwhelmed. He had given me an instruction to go and tell everyone about him, but, more importantly, he had called me his 'son'.

I went into that church a sinner, and came out a saint; and I *knew* that I had been born again. I felt like a new man. My desperation left me, and the Lord put a lightness in my spirit that has never left me. I knew Jesus was for real. At last, I knew it was true. I also knew my life would never be the same again. My life was transformed instantly, and I wanted to tell everyone about Jesus.

When we returned to the pub, I turned the music off, and told everyone in the bar that they would go to hell unless they were born again. I think I gave a few people indigestion that Sunday lunchtime! Thora took me aside, and told me that was not how we were supposed to win people over for Christ. She started to pray for sensitivity for me. Fifteen years later, I am still waiting for it to arrive!

I had met with Jesus, and received him as my Lord and Saviour, but I still had an ailing business, and was desperate.

The following weeks were so painful. I was bankrupt, and we lost everything. Not only was bankruptcy a terribly humiliating process, but I was also consumed with anxiety for my family. I had to borrow £115 to apply for a bankruptcy order. I crawled into the court feeling ashamed, and so aware that I was letting a lot of people down. We were so hard up that I even had to borrow the money for the petrol to get me there. Whilst I was in court, I was issued with a parking ticket for more than the car was worth. I thought that I would die of shame.

We eventually left the pub and moved into a council house. I did whatever job came my way, refusing to claim state benefit, as I knew God would provide for us—and he did. Following my conversion, I was invited to give my testimony in churches, at FGBMFI (Full Gospel Businessmen's Fellowship International) dinners, in prisons and schools. I was almost as much a celebrity as I had been during my footballing days, but this time my motives were very different. Instead of 'saving goals', my goal was now to see souls saved. When I met with the Lord in the Baptist church that Sunday morning, he gave me a passion for Jesus that I cannot contain. I am overwhelmed by the knowledge that people will go to hell unless they have Jesus in their lives. Often, I meet people I will never see again, so I feel conscious that I have one opportunity to tell them the truth; and to lead them to Jesus, who alone can save them from an eternity in hell.

My conversion took place fifteen years ago, and my love and passion for Jesus have gone from strength to strength. Often, I recall my days as a footballer. I endured a huge amount of verbal abuse from fans, and that proved to be a good training ground for my life as an evangelist and missionary. When people mock, and scorn me for my faith, it is like 'water off a duck's back'. It does not bother me at all: I have a message to proclaim. Jesus himself asked me to tell everyone about him, so I do. It is that simple. He called, and I answered; every day he gives me the strength and grace to take his message to strangers. Since the day I met with him, I have not looked back. I have never felt spiritually low; I have never felt I did not want to read the Bible or pray; nor have I, at any time, felt unable to talk about Jesus. That is nothing to do with *my* strength; it is the grace of God which keeps me going. Asking the Lord Jesus into my life was the most satisfying thing I have ever done. I was a man who had the best things that money could buy, but all that pales into insignificance, compared with what I have now.

These days, I work for the Lord as a full time evangelist. I travel all over the world, proclaiming his love and salvation. I am so grateful he chose me for the life I now have, and for blessing me with a godly wife, who prayed for me to know the Lord Jesus. Nothing compares to the joy of watching someone give his or her life to Jesus.

Jesus told me not to be frightened, because he was with me; from that day to this, he has kept his promise.

4

Thora Tindall

Before I became a Christian, my life was an emotional 'roller-coaster'. After Mike left professional football, our financial security was, at times, fragile and this had a huge effect upon our marriage. From being well off, we found ourselves having to be more careful. We had both worked really hard and enjoyed the rewards, only to have them snatched away. It was emotionally and physically exhausting.

Things were quite bad between us. It now seems amazing that we survived those years together. I suppose the children kept me with Mike, but I have to acknowledge that, even then, God had his hand on us; though we had no idea what that was to mean.

Over the years, I became bogged down with being a wife, mother and businesswoman, and it finally took its toll on my health. Mike did not understand what was happening to me. He was oblivious to the fact that I had brought a lot of 'baggage' into our marriage, which affected my capacity to give and receive love from him.

I felt as if I was locked in a loveless marriage, and considered divorcing Mike, but I did not have the emotional resources to go through with it. My insecurity, in those days, stemmed from the fact that my mother had died when I was fifteen. Following her funeral, I was told that the woman I had called 'mother' all my life was in fact my grandmother. I was shocked to discover that my 'sister' was really my birth mother. In an instant, my life changed; I was devastated. I was not the person I had thought myself to be. Now I questioned the trustworthiness of my family, as well as my identity. Consequently, I did not feel 'whole'. Those discoveries about my family affected my ability to give or receive love freely. I remember often asking myself, 'Why am I here?'

Meeting Mike was wonderful; we had such a fun-filled and privileged lifestyle; but years of suppressing my emotions took its toll on our relationship. Long before giving my life to Jesus, I started to ask God about my childhood, and told him how I felt. I was in the bath one day, and asked God if his love for me was as great as the Bible says it is. As I stepped out of the bath and wrapped myself in a towel, I felt God wrap his love around me. In an instant, I felt clean —totally accepted and loved. Right there and then, God delivered me from a sea of anxiety and depression. All the questions I had ever asked myself about God were answered in that steamy bathroom. I knew where I had come from, why I was here, and where I was going; I felt like a brand new person, and, from that day to this, I never looked back. Although Mike and I had difficult times again, I would never again feel alone. Everything now seemed different. My capacity to love, and to be loved, increased overnight. I noticed a difference in our marriage almost immediately.

My life and marriage were totally transformed. The moment I asked Jesus into my life, he gave me a fresh love for Mike; and the more Jesus tidied up my life, the more my capacity to love Mike increased.

Looking back, I cannot even begin to comprehend the miracle God has worked in our relationship. I am completely overwhelmed at how the Lord has blessed us. Not only do I love Mike passionately, but he is also my best friend and 'soul mate'. Anyone who has been locked in a difficult marriage will tell you that, even with the best will in the world, it is impossible to 'work up' those feelings, once you have lost them. It is not that I have brought about the change: the Lord Jesus has! He healed me of my emotional 'baggage', and he healed my marriage. Not a bad swop: my problems for his love. It is amazing! But I did not suddenly become a perfect wife. I had to work on my attitude towards Mike, and I knew that I still had a choice: either I could accept the love Jesus gave me for Mike, and change my attitude towards him, or I could carry on as I was. Having spent years believing that I felt nothing for my husband, I knew he would take some convincing that I felt differently towards him. Making a conscious decision to become a 'doormat' for Mike, I tried hard to be the best wife possible. I stopped wanting things my way all the time. I cooked him lovely meals, and spent time listening to him. It was a struggle sometimes—because, in a sense, I was still the old Thora—but with God's help I just did everything to the best of my ability. I accepted Mike for what he was, and the only things I commented on were those I found deeply offensive, like bad language.

I constantly called out to the Lord in prayer for Mike, and only had to wait two years for him to become a Christian. But that was an intense time. I cried out to God night and day for him. Without my fully understanding what had happened to me, the Lord blessed me with the gift of intercession, and I spent hours on my knees for Mike. My first prayer in the morning, as I awoke, was for my husband. I prayed it as regularly as I cleaned my teeth: "Lord, I praise you and bless you, and I just want to bring my husband before you this day." That would start me off on a torrent of prayer for him. The thought of hell terrified me, and I could not bear the thought of Mike going there. I vividly recall telling God, on many occasions, that I did not care what the cost would be. He was to do whatever it took to bring Mike to his knees. I told the Lord that he could take every penny we had; I would be a tramp on the street, if only he would save Mike. I never thought we would get so close!

Most of the time, Mike did not object to my faith, because life had improved so much for him. I was a much better wife and mother, apart from irritating him when I spoke to other people about Jesus! Looking back, I realise I must have driven him nuts, because I was always talking about Jesus to people; I could not help myself.

Through attending a Bible study group, I learnt about the vital importance of forgiveness, and I made a conscious decision to forgive Mike for everything he had ever said and done to hurt me. It was not easy, but I wanted to be obedient to God, and I would have done anything to lead Mike to Christ. I also asked for forgiveness for not being the wife to Mike that I should have been. God gave me the strength and grace to forgive Mike and not return to the past. So I moved on as a Christian wife, and I believe that was an important part of my walk with the Lord. The Bible says you have to be a witness; I knew that God had blessed me and helped me to grow as I let go of past hurts. The more I forgave, the more love God gave me for Mike.

I attended a weekly prayer group in church, and prayed for Mike. Scores of Christians prayed for him on a regular basis, and I met with another Christian woman once a week, to pray for our unsaved husbands. Eventually, both of them gave their lives to the Lord. During the hours I spent in prayer for Mike, I would become very emotional, weeping for him. Often, I would do this in church meetings when we prayed for Mike, and I would be so embarrassed that I almost wanted to die with shame. I could not control the depth of despair I felt for him. It was a dear Christian friend who explained that what was growing in me was something called the gift of intercession. The tears and groaning I uttered were biblical. There was no stopping me after that!

Members of the Baptist church at Lansdown, Bournemouth, were elated for me when I was born again, and began attending church as a believer. When Mike announced he wanted to buy a pub, I was horrified. As a child, I had seen what drink did to people's lives, and felt that as a Christian I could not be in that trade. The church started to pray for me, encouraging me to trust in the Lord. I had only been a Christian for a few weeks, and could not believe God would now want me to be a publican. I wrestled with the thought endlessly, until one night I called out to God to help me. I then had a clear picture of the inside of a pub, with lights and music, and I knew that we would move to the pub in Bromsgrove. It could not have been any clearer; in my mind's eye I could see a ticker tape with the words, "That's where I want you, Thora," written over and over again. It certainly was not what I wanted to hear, but I decided not to argue against God. If he wanted me to be a pub landlady, then he would somehow use it for good.

Unbeknown to me, two hundred miles away, Christians in Bromsgrove had been praying for the pub we were about to move to. It was a local trouble spot, and caused a great deal of concern in the community. I think they were praying for the pub to close down. Little did they know that God would answer their prayers in such an unusual way!

I did not enjoy being involved in running the pub, but always found a way to talk about Jesus to the customers. We had a massive clientele of young, vibrant people. They all knew how I felt about the Lord and, miraculously, accepted me as I was. I prayed continually for Mike, and for all the people with whom we came into contact in the pub. I did not waste one single opportunity to point out to people that drink was not the answer to their problems —Jesus was!

Following our move to Bromsgrove, I joined New Road Baptist Church, and they were hugely supportive to me, committing themselves to pray for Mike regularly. The whole church was primed to pray for Mike; every time one of the congregation walked past the pub, the Lord would prompt them to pray for Mike's salvation. As the pub was on the High Street, he was on the receiving end of an enormous amount of prayer, on a daily basis.

About a year before Mike was born again, he became foul-mouthed. The worse his behaviour became, the more I prayed; calling on other Christians to pray for him, too. It was such a difficult time for me, and living with him was really hard; it would have been so easy to run away, but I hung on, knowing that God would be faithful to all the prayers of his people for Mike. God was so gracious. I used to cry out to him for Mike, as if my heart would break. I would go into the bedroom, pound on my pillow and cry out to God to help me, and to save my husband! I would become so angry about Mike's behaviour. I did not know how to deal with him, nor what my response should be to his antics. I wanted to be a good witness to Mike, and called out to God endlessly for his strength and grace to cope. It was such a physically exhausting time. I was so grateful for the support of the Christians in my church, and would not have got through that time without them.

Whilst I was praying for Mike, the Lord was working in my life too, dealing with past hurts and insecurities. Developing severe pre-menstrual tension added to the agony—both for myself and Mike. Looking back, I recognise that as having been the time of the last battle for Mike, before he was born again. Yet my behaviour was so appalling: for a while, I had no control over my words or actions. I became physically violent, and started throwing things—anything that came to hand. We can laugh about it now, but at the time it was awful. I remember waiting for Mike to join us for Christmas lunch. The children and I waited at the table for an hour, whilst he pottered around in the bar, preparing for the evening opening. Mike would get so involved with the pub; he has always been a sociable man, and once he got chatting he was unable to stop. I had told him that lunch was ready, but he forgot! By the time he came upstairs, the lunch was ruined and I was fit to explode. As he walked through the door, I threw his plate at him. I remember staring at a turkey leg hanging off the wall clock! I couldn't believe what I had done, and neither could the rest of the family! Then I was convinced Mike would never come to the Lord because of my behaviour. So much for being an ambassador for Christ!

When I was not 'freaking out' due to spiralling hormone levels, I continued acting as a 'doormat' for Mike. I had learnt about the persecuted church, and felt that my suffering was nothing compared to theirs. Throughout the world, people suffered great loss, and some even died for their faith; so surely I could cope with Mike. The Lord asked me, "Can I trust you with a bit of hardship, without your falling away?" I knew he could, and I persevered, praying constantly for Mike's salvation, and for God's strength to cope.

Shortly before Mike was born again, I had a 'run in' with God. I had been witnessing to a non-Christian friend for a long time, and felt I had invested a lot of time in her. I had encouraged her to attend church, and spent hours talking about Jesus to her. I knew she would soon give her life to the Lord, and looked forward to leading her through the prayer of commitment. One particular Sunday, someone else took my friend to church. During the service, she asked the Lord into her life. Instead of being thrilled, I was miffed that I had not been the one to lead her to that point. I told God, in no un-certain terms, that I did not like the way he worked. It just was not fair that I had done all the groundwork, yet someone else had swept in and led my friend to the Lord. I felt the Lord speak very clearly to me; he asked me if I was ready to 'play second fiddle'. At the time I did not really understand the significance of God's question, but I knew instantly that my attitude was wrong. I felt so ashamed of my response, and immediately repented. That was a huge lesson in humility. On that day, I learnt that some of us sow the seeds of faith, some plant, some tend; and some reap the harvest of souls. We rarely do the lot ourselves. We all have a role to play, and it is up to God to choose our part, not us.

Following Mike's conversion, I understood what the Lord had meant about 'playing second fiddle'. For so long, I had been the centre of attention in the church family. Once Mike gave his heart to the Lord, we started attending church to-gether as a believing couple; then all the attention focused on him. I was no longer in charge. My husband would take spir-itual leadership in our home, and I had to adjust to my new role as 'second fiddle'! Overnight, I willingly learnt to make that adjustment.

Mike has gone from strength to strength: he is a wonderful

evangelist, and the Lord has led us into the most amazing ministry together.

All the prayers and tears for my husband were worth it. God has answered me, beyond my wildest dreams. He healed our marriage and enriched our lives beyond measure. I am sure that one of the essential factors in Mike's being born again was the fact that I was willing to let the Lord change *me*. Though I did not know it at the time, Mike was stunned by the transformation in me. My whole life did a complete 180° turn, and I give God all the glory, because he faithfully heard and answered all the prayers for my husband, blessing us so much.

I can easily identify several areas that the Lord worked on in my life, as he worked on Mike. I had to learn to forgive people for my past, and, just as importantly, receive and accept forgiveness myself, and trust Jesus. I went on believing for Mike's salvation, and tried to be a witness to him by the way I lived. I called upon Christian brothers and sisters to support me in prayer for him. When I was struggling, I asked them to pray for me personally, for strength to continue. When I was strong, I went into 'prayer overdrive'. Mike Tindall was saturated in prayer, offered by people he had never met, from the day I was born again until the day he gave his life to the Lord. No wonder God moved powerfully in our lives!

When we married, I thought we had it all; yet what we may have had then pales into insignificance, in comparison with what we have now.

5

Glenn Titley

"My friends would describe me as a man's man: a fun loving man of high morals. I enjoy family life, football, golf, and a pint with the lads."

My family only attended church for weddings, funerals, and christenings. Mum was raised a Catholic, but I do not remember her going to mass, and we did not go as children. I think dad would describe himself as "Church of England", if pushed. I suppose we are typical of many families in Britain today, considering ourselves Christian because we are decent, hard working people.

When I was twelve years old, my nineteen year old cousin, Tommy, developed cancer and died. His illness and death had a big effect on the family. I think it was during that time I remember religion being mentioned in our home. A lot of anger was directed towards God. Why would he allow such a dreadful thing to happen to Tommy, hurting all of us? No one had anything good to say about God or called on him in prayer, as far as I remember.

From the age of eleven, I attended the Boy's Brigade with

a friend. It was a good social scene and we did a lot of fun stuff. It kept us off the streets and on the straight and narrow. In order to take part in the recreational activities, we had to attend compulsory church services. So we used to trot off to the local church, dressed up in our uniforms, flag in hand, and daydream throughout the services. It was a small price to pay to notch up more points towards yet another badge for my uniform. At the time, it did not seem to mean anything to me, but looking back now, I think that something was 'drip feeding' into me. We did hear the Bible read every week. But, as far as I was concerned, it was simply a means to an end.

After I left the Boys Brigade, I became a bit of a 'jack the lad'. I was always out with friends having a good time, only just managing to stay out of serious trouble. Happily for me, I met Susan. She was a lovely girl, and began to have a great influence on my life. We soon fell in love, and I decided I wanted to spend the rest of my life with her. We started planning our wedding. I still went out with friends and had a good time, but now felt secure in the knowledge that Susan was there for me. We set a date to marry, and started looking for a church. Susan's parish church refused to marry us as we were not attenders, so we went to St. Leonard's, Frankley. That was where we met Michael Denny, the Vicar, who shattered my stereotypical image of vicars. It was delightful to discover someone who was lively, great fun, a 'decent bloke' —and far from the 'oddball' image of Christians I had previously held. He agreed to marry us, providing we would attend marriage preparation classes. During that time, we discussed every aspect of sharing life with another person —from emotional responses to family planning. It was a really useful course, and we both enjoyed going along each week. We got on well with Michael, and I felt comfortable attending church to hear our wedding banns read. Apart from enjoying Michael's company and the course content, I really was not interested in religion at all. I was happy with my life, and had no need of God. He was for weak people, not someone like me, a 'macho' man!

After we married, we lost contact with the church. I felt I had done my bit and could get on with life. A few years went by; we moved to Stoke Prior, and Susan started to go to the local parish church. I had no desire to go with her, so she went alone. I had plenty of friends at work and in the village and was content to let Susan do her own thing, as long as it didn't affect me. She became a regular church attender. This did not affect me at all, until one night she went to a Graham Kendrick concert. She came home beaming, saying that she asked Jesus into her life. She became what I would call a devoted Christian almost immediately. She went to church as often as she could, always had her nose in the Bible, and devoured Christian books. Every time I came home, there would be 'Jesus music' booming through the house. Suddenly, my home and my wife had been taken over by everything Christian! I think I was in a state of disbelief. I could not understand why she was not content with just going to church now and again. Instead of quietly getting on with life, she suddenly seemed to me to have become a fanatic.

When something like that happens, it is very hard to understand, as a non-Christian. Susan did try to explain to me what was happening, but I suppose I had selective deafness. I just could not 'get my head around' the full picture. I remember her telling me she had fallen in love with Jesus! I was stunned. When your wife says she has fallen for another man, even though it is someone who has been dead for two thousand years, it is quite threatening. I had always come first in her life; now she was telling me that had changed. I had no idea how to deal with this unseen rival, so I rebelled. I felt pushed out, so I decided to spend more time with people who had time for me. I went out drinking far more often, and stayed out late. I knew it annoyed her, but I really believed that she was happy doing her thing and I could be happy doing mine. Looking back, I know that was an unworkable and dangerous situation to be in. I think that if it had gone on any longer than it did, it probably would have split us up. There were times I could see that what I was doing was wrong; yet I still rebelled. It seems so silly now, because I knew with all my heart that, even though she loved the Lord, I also knew she still loved me as much as she had always done.

Susan left the parish church and joined a Baptist church. Fairly quickly, she became involved with the Sunday school. She took her commitment very seriously, and would spend hours preparing activities for the children. I saw this as a huge invasion of my space. Whilst she was preparing classes, I would become angry and resentful. I was jealous, and felt she should be sitting with me, not reading her Bible or praying. I wanted to be the most important thing in her life. But of course, being a 'macho' man, I never told her this.

As our children grew up, they would ask me to go to special family services with them. I was proud of my children, and family time was important to me. Finding myself unable to say 'no' to them, I would often accept their invitations when I was not working. Every time I went to church, the people I met were, again, very different to the picture I had of 'oddball Christians'. The men were friendly, and seemed normal. I always expected someone to pounce on me and 'Bible bash'. Much to my surprise, they never did. We would talk about football, kids and the weather; but I was always on my guard, just in case someone tried to convert me. I was a 'real man', determined to prove to them I did not need God. I believed in making my own destiny; I certainly did not need someone else to do it for me. Only weak, inadequate people, with no inner strength, believed in God. I had learnt to rely on no one, except Glenn Titley.

One evening, we were invited to a church supper. I had met Mike Tindall a few times, and always doubly braced myself for a Bible bashing, because I knew he was unrelenting in his pursuit of converts. I tolerated him, because talking about Jesus was his job. As an evangelist, he never missed an opportunity to slip Jesus into the conversation. I had no intention of becoming another spiritual notch on his belt. Mike came over and started to chat about Jesus. I listened to what he had to say, simply because I did not want to be rude. However, I told him quite firmly that I was not interested. I was happy as I was, and advised him to save his speech for somebody else. However, I knew right there and then that some of the things he said to me rang alarm bells in the back of my head. But I certainly was not going to tell him that!

In November 1995, Mike decided to have another crack at converting me. I looked him straight in the eye and told him, "I'm not ready."

With absolute confidence, he looked me straight in the eye and said, "You will be soon, Glenn." His confidence caught me off guard, and I struggled to shrug off his comments as wishful thinking on his part.

One month later, on the 17th December, we went to a Christmas service at the New Road Baptist Church. Susan had invited her family, as well as my parents and sisters. The candlelit service was beautiful. It was the first time I had ever enjoyed a church service. Suddenly, I felt comfortable; it seemed right for me to be there, and I felt completely at home.

After the service, we said goodbye to our family and went our separate ways. I followed my usual Sunday night routine, which was to go out for a drink with friends. The pub was about a mile away from home; there were no street lights between the edge of the village and the pub car park. I enjoyed the walk. It was a beautiful night, and I had enjoyed a good weekend, so I was in great form, but something made me decide not to remain in the pub but to go back home. The night was so still and clear. I strode out back towards the village in pitch darkness, then saw a street light in the distance. As I walked along the dark country lane, I started to reflect on the service earlier that evening. The sermon had been about light and dark, good and evil. As I walked, I was aware that I was in the dark, walking towards the light. Suddenly, I noticed that the street lamp on the edge of the village was much brighter than usual: abnormally bright; and, as I got closer, I could almost feel heat from the bulb, it was so bright. I assumed it was a power surge, and expected the bulb to pop at any moment. As I walked underneath the lamp, a voice in my head said, "Glenn, come and kneel before me." I was so surprised that I stopped and looked around. I laughed out loud, told myself I was going barmy, and walked on. As I walked out of the light into the gloom again, I heard the voice once more. "Glenn, come and kneel before me." This time, I turned around and walked slowly back into the light. As I walked back, there were a hundred voices in my head, telling me not to go back. Each voice was taunting,

"You'll lose all your friends."

"You'll never be the same."

"You'll end up as one of those wacky Christians."

"No one will want to know you."

The voices tormented me; but I still went back. The brightness of the lamp was awesome: something supernatural was happening, not just with the lamp, but inside my heart, too. Right there and then, in the middle of the village, I had heard Jesus call to me to kneel before him. So I did! I knew what to do, having heard it often enough from Susan, Mike Tindall and, that night, in church. I knelt on the pavement and gave Jesus my life; I simply asked him to forgive me for all my sins, and come into my life.

As I prayed, I had a tangible physical experience. It was rather like the feeling you have when you are cold, and shudder from top to toe; but rather than being an uncomfortable, creepy feeling, it was the exact opposite. I felt a warm, loving peace flow through my body, and it seemed to run down my back. Then I started to weep. At that moment, I felt so clean, and so totally loved.

I do not know how long I was there; it could have been minutes or hours. I was oblivious of time, and was aware only of the presence of God. I realised then that it was past closing time, because someone I knew, returning from the pub, found me in tears, sitting under the street lamp. By this time, I was in quite an emotional state, and he thought I had been attacked. I told him what had happened, and that I had asked the Lord into my life. I expected him to be shocked, but for some reason he was not. He simply said, "It will probably be the most important decision you'll ever make in your life, mate."

By the time I returned home, I was sobbing uncontrollably, and I could barely tell Susan what had happened. Once
I managed to explain, we both started bawling our eyes out.

I had no idea what to do; I was in a state of shock. I had
only gone out with the intention of having a quiet drink with
my mates. Two hours later, I was a sobbing wreck, having
asked Jesus into my life! Sue called in the cavalry, and rang
Mike Tindall. The one man I had tried to avoid for so long
was the one man I now wanted to see. I knew that he would
be able to make sense of what was happening to me.

Mike got out of his bed in the middle of the night, to talk
and pray with me. For the first time in my life, I really spoke
to God: it felt so right. At last, all this Christianity business
made sense. I now understood what had happened to Susan
after the Graham Kendrick concert, all those years ago.
I cried, on and off, for three days. I was so grateful that I was
on annual leave. A blubbering Glenn Titley would have done
nothing for my 'street cred'!

A few days before my conversion, Susan had brought a
videotape home, and asked me to watch it. She would often
bring things home for me to look at, in an effort to convert
me; and she usually got the same response from me, "I'm not
interested." Anyway, I was home with my son, Joshua, during
the Christmas holidays; there was nothing we wanted to
watch on the television, and Josh was getting bored.
I remembered the video Susan had brought home, and decided we would watch it, to amuse Josh. The video was the
testimony of an Australian man, who was stung by a deadly
box jellyfish. His story was amazing, and really touched my
heart. I wept uncontrollably throughout the video. I cannot
remember whether Joshua was more taken with the video or
me.

From that day, I became hungry for more knowledge of
Jesus. I could not wait to buy a Bible of my own. Having
bought it, I then wanted to read it all in one go. I started going to church, and really felt at peace with myself and with
Jesus. My conversion was so dramatic that I was asked to give
my testimony in church. I was really scared as I thought

people would think I was wacky, drunk or mentally ill. I knew that I was none of these, so I stood up in church and told my story. I had such a furnace burning inside me for the Lord. I just wanted to honour him, and encourage other people.

Before my conversion, I could not understand why Susan wanted to go to church twice on a Sunday. She would go to the morning service with the children, and then to the evening service on her own, leaving me to babysit. I used to go mad, because I wanted to be with my mates in the pub. She would get home about 8.45 p.m. I would demand to know what she had been doing until that time. It was beyond me why she wanted to spend so much time in church; it was not normal! Following my conversion, we would fight as to whose turn it was to go to church in the evening. Suddenly, I loved being in church, and was so hungry to learn more. Nowadays, I would go to church three times a day if I could.

When I was a child, my parents instilled their values in me; boundaries, and moral codes of behaviour were set. As I grew up, I had adapted their codes to suit myself, making my own 'ground rules'. Since I began to study the Bible, my understanding of right behaviour is more clearly defined. There are no 'grey areas' in life. One either chooses to live by God's rules —or not. The surprising thing is that it is not difficult to live by God's rules. In fact, it is easier.

Since becoming a Christian, I am a much better husband and father. I am more caring and loving, and able to show my feelings. I work long days—often six or seven days a week. I would often come home weary, desperate for some peace and quiet, only to find the children squabbling and demanding. This was often difficult for me. I coped with it by retreating to the pub for a pint. Nowadays, I deal with the children differently: no more running away to the pub. I am not a perfect husband and father, but I am aware that I now have an inbuilt 'braking system'. I know how to respond more appropriately, without the help of a pint of beer.

My greatest fear about becoming a Christian, before I met the Lord personally, was that I would lose my friends. God knew that this was so, and has honoured my friendships, which happily it has been possible to maintain. My friends are quite comfortable with my faith. I try not to 'ram Christianity down their throats'. I know that 'Bible bashing' turned me off, and it would them, as well. In a way, I see myself as a 'friendship evangelist'. My friends know that I am here for them, which is very important to me. Occasionally, I invite friends to church concerts and special events, and, out of respect for me, they accept my invitations. I am aware it is quite a big thing for them to do, and appreciate their response to my faith.

In matters of faith, it seems that men are often harder to reach than women. Women tend to be more open, taking things at face value, whereas men tend to need proof of God's existence. I believe that if we tried to reach men with the evidence, stressing the historical facts about Jesus Christ, his life and resurrection, we would be much more effective in evangelism.

I thought that my friends would be the hardest people to tell about my new found faith, but that was not the case. Surprisingly, I found it extremely difficult to talk to some of my relatives, though they know what I believe, and occasionally come to concerts and Christmas services. It is very difficult to have such a 'no go' area with people you love, and I now know how Susan felt for all those years!

My fears—of becoming a religious nut, and losing my friends—were unfounded. Belonging to the church has meant more than just attending services; running a youth group for teenagers and welcoming people on the door are among the ways in which I am privileged to serve God. I know that I am more approachable now, and really care about others. I have been told that I have the gift of hospitality. I make people feel at ease, and can talk to them. I now have a burning desire for Jesus to use me to make a positive difference in other people's lives. I have a lot to give, and God will show me how to use my compassion.

The rewards of being a Christian are too numerous to

put into words. The main one for me is that, with God on my side, there is no need to worry about things. He is only a prayer away. I have seen some amazing answers to prayer, which have strengthened my faith in him. A short time after I became a Christian, someone very close to me was seriously ill and nearly died. Sue and I, and many Christian friends, went into 'prayer overdrive' for God to save her —and he did. I do not know why God chose not to save my cousin Tommy's life all those years ago, but I do know that he chose to listen to my prayers on this occasion. I have absolute faith that God listens to every word we pray.

Looking back, I realise Susan has made such an impact on my life. At times, I made her life a misery. I knew what I was doing was wrong, but it was as if I were incapable of controlling my attitude and behaviour towards her. So often, I would push for a reaction from her. I pushed and pushed her to the limit. The odd thing was, the more I pushed, the more she failed to respond to my goading. Time and time again, she proved her love for me. Eventually, I came to the realisation that if I was not going to get a reaction I might as well stop behaving badly.

Susan told me that she and a group of friends prayed for me regularly. I felt a mixture of emotions about this. Initially it felt weird; it seemed so invasive. But then I felt very special, knowing that people were spending time praying for me. I am convinced that persistent intercessory prayer is used by God to save people.

Jesus means everything to me. He is my life, and I cannot imagine life without him. Even if, for some reason, I stopped going to church, it would not change the way I feel about Jesus. I cannot foresee ever losing the bond we have formed. Before becoming a Christian, I was so frightened of ridicule; of being perceived as weak, or 'not quite right in the head'. I cannot encourage people enough to stop listening to their own and others' doubts: they are totally unfounded. I am more of a man now than I have ever been. I am still Glenn Titley, but a better version!

One of my favourite scriptures is Psalm 103:11–13,

**For as high as the heavens are above the earth,
so great is his love for those who fear him;
As far as the east is from the west,
so far he has removed our transgressions from us.**

I experienced God's awesome love and forgiveness for me, just as the scripture promises.

The Lord knows your heart, your fears and your worries. The time to put your life right with him is always the present. I became aware of his presence and call to repentance, under a street lamp in the middle of Stoke Prior. I know, without a shadow of doubt, that accepting Jesus into my life is a decision I will never regret. Jesus enriched my life beyond measure. If I were to give anybody advice, it would be this: do not hold back; there is no need to be afraid. Make sure you respond to his call; do not miss out on the best choice, as you make the greatest decision of your life.

6

Sue Titley

"Ask and it will be given to you; seek and you will find; knock and the door will be opened to you. For everyone who asks receives; he who seeks finds; and to him who knocks, the door will be opened."

Luke 11:9b–10

I think that I became a Christian when attending Sunday school. My mother tells me that, as a very young child, I would talk to God as if he were in the room with me. My parents were not themselves religious and, with the passage of time, my faith seemed to evaporate. But I did retain an awareness that God was real. Eventually, I met Glenn and fell head over heels in love with him. Although I had not made an adult commitment to God, I knew that, in a sense, life with Glenn and life with God were incompatible; so I rejected God and chose Glenn.

Through the years, God brought me into contact with a number of Christians, but I think the first one who really touched my life was the same person who was to make such an impression on Glenn: Michael Denny, the vicar who married us—a remarkable man. He lived his life honourably, and was great fun. He made a tremendous impression on us and rekindled my childhood interest in God. Following our wedding, I desperately wanted to go to church, but Glenn was so unhappy about it that I did not bother, and did not mention religion again until we moved to Stoke Prior. Once we had settled into our new home, I took my courage in both hands and started going to the parish church. It was very traditional and not very challenging. I undertook a confirmation course, and it was actually during my confirmation service that I fell in love with the Lord and asked Jesus into my life. I felt so strongly that I wanted Glenn to understand that I was serious about God that I asked him to come to the classes with me. Interestingly, Glenn did not mention the confirmation course in his testimony. It was a very special time for me, but an absolute non-event for Glenn.

I was very quiet about my faith for a long time, as I did not want to upset Glenn. Little did I know that things were about to change dramatically.

The Parish Church appointed a lady vicar, Margaret Smallman. I immediately recognised there was something different about her faith. Her relationship with God seemed more intense. There was a power in her faith that I knew I lacked. She explained that it was the presence of the Holy Spirit in her life. For the first time, I learnt that the Holy Spirit was a Person, and he governed her relationship with Jesus. I could not understand what she was talking about, but I acknowledged the difference between her faith and mine. I was so hungry for more of God, but did not know what to do about it.

Some months after I met Margaret, she organised an outing to a Graham Kendrick concert. I loved his music and looked forward to hearing him play live. On the day of the concert, I was very ill with a tummy bug; but I was nonetheless determined to go. Glenn was really angry with me for wanting to go to the concert, as I looked so ill. He asked me not to go, but I knew I had to be there. After the concert had finished, there was a call for anyone who wanted to receive the in-filling of the Holy Spirit, to stand up. I was on my feet in an instant; but was quite defiant in my attitude towards God, saying to him, "Okay, I don't understand this Holy Spirit business, so you had better show me what it's all about." When I stood, some people on the ministry team came over and started to pray for me. I was aware that people were laying hands on me. As they did so, I felt an amazing bolt of energy and power shoot through my body. It was like an electric shock, but without the pain. I had a very clear picture of Jesus on the cross, asking me to 'forgive myself' for things that I had done in my life. I saw very clearly that each time I dragged up past hurt and guilt, I was hammering the nails into Jesus afresh. Jesus had forgiven me, so I now had to forgive others and to accept myself as forgiven by him, too. I felt an amazing sense of love and peace, and I knew we would spend eternity together. At that point, I simply started worshipping Jesus. Suddenly, my self-consciousness melted away, and I started praying. I was so surprised by this, as I had never dared to pray aloud in church, as I was so shy.

When I arrived home, Glenn could see the difference in me. Some time later, he told me that I 'radiated'. I had left the house feeling and looking ill, and returned a new woman. He was taken aback, and quite frightened of the change in me. Because Glenn was my best friend, and we shared everything, it seemed natural that I should share my experience with him, so I spilled my heart out. I bubbled over with enthusiasm, and told him I had fallen in love with Jesus in a new and deeper way, and that I felt my life was never going to be the same again. I also told him that I loved him, and knew that the devil would try and attack our marriage. With hindsight, I did a lot of damage that night. Glenn was absolutely shell-shocked, and struggled to make sense of what was happening to me. I was completely unaware that my enthusiasm scared him to death. Initially, his behaviour towards me did not change at all. He let me get on with my life, and he got on with his. I did not realise what a dangerous situation we were creating.

The following Christmas, Glenn bought me a beautiful Bible. I was so touched that he had made the effort to acknowledge my faith. Not only had he thought of me and bought the gift, but he had thumbed through the Bible, to inscribe the following words:

To Sue, presented by Glenn Titley
on the occasion of the birthday of Jesus Christ.
This is the message we have heard from him and declare to you: God is light; in him there is no darkness at all. If we claim to have fellowship with him yet walk in the darkness, we lie and do not live by the truth. But if we walk in the light, as he is in the light, we have fellowship with one another, and the blood of Jesus, his Son, purifies us from all sin.

I John 1:5–8

I was amazed that my anti-Christian husband had searched the Bible and chosen a passage of scripture for me. Such a huge act of kindness and love carried me through many testing times in our relationship.

That was Christmas 1989; during the next few years we gradually began to go our separate ways. As I became more involved with church activities, Glenn started to go out more with his friends. Often, he returned home in the early hours of the morning, after spending the night in clubs. He was reluctant to talk to me about his friends, and their times together. Christianity was definitely a 'no go' area. He used to get very angry when I prepared work for the Sunday school classes. In order to keep the peace, I retreated to the bedroom, thinking I was doing the right thing. I was oblivious to the fact that I was merely inflaming the situation by not being with him. His moods darkened, and his behaviour towards me became quite vile; he seemed so angry with me most of the time. When my Christian friends telephoned or visited our home, he would become enraged. He worked long hours, and we never seemed to spend time together as a family. I felt unsupported and very alone. I missed my husband terribly; he had been my best friend for so long. I was hurt that he wanted to spend so much time with his friends. Little did I realise how much I was hurting him. As far as I was concerned, my love for Jesus had increased my love for Glenn. Unbeknown to me, Glenn felt that I loved him less, and had more time for Christian friends and activities than I did for him. I just did not realise that he believed another man had replaced him: an unseen, unreachable rival had stolen my heart from him.

Glenn's heart seemed so hard towards God that I was reminded of the conversion of Saul. He had been so anti-Christian that he made it his mission in life to persecute followers of Jesus Christ. His passion in life was to kill believers. However, the risen Jesus met with him on the road to Damascus, and asked Saul why he was persecuting him. So dramatic was his meeting with Jesus, that his ways changed immediately, and God made him the apostle and evangelist who would be instrumental in taking the good news to the Gentile world. I remember asking God to give Glenn a similar experience to that which Saul had undergone, and to change Glenn's life. I knew it would take something dramatic to melt my husband's heart. I prayed for a 'road to Damascus' experience for him. Every time he went out with his friends, I would put the children to bed and settle down to read the Bible and pray. I always asked the Lord to protect my husband, and bring him home safely. One verse that meant a lot to me was Matthew 6:6,

"When you pray, go into your room, close the door and pray to your Father, who is unseen. Then your Father, who sees what is done in secret, will reward you."

Jesus also showed me that I had to forgive Glenn for his behaviour towards me.

"...For if you forgive men when they sin against you, your heavenly Father will also forgive you."

Matthew: 6:14

On one particular occasion, I remember meeting a friend to pray, and I returned home later than expected. When I arrived back home, Glenn was waiting at the door, eager to go out with his friends. He was so angry with me that, for the first time in our marriage, I felt frightened; it just was not my Glenn. It was like looking into the face of a stranger—and an evil one, at that. After he had left the house, I fell on my knees and called out to God for his help. I felt that my whole life was falling apart; my husband was becoming a stranger, and the tension in our home was unbearable. I just could not carry on any more.

Whilst I was praying, I thought of the story of the prodigal son, and remembered the suffering of the father as he had allowed his son to leave him. I felt that God was telling me to release Glenn to him, stop worrying, and delight in Jesus. In the same way that the prodigal son returned to his father, so Glenn would return to me. God had the whole matter in hand, and I had to trust him. The verse that came to mind was, **'Delight yourself in the LORD and he will give you the desires of your heart'** (Psalm 37:4).

I realised, then, that my faith was causing Glenn so much distress that I needed to be more sensitive to his needs, withdrawing from church activities and spending more time in God's presence. I gave up teaching Sunday school and prayer meetings, and simply attended the Sunday services. I did not know how I would survive, giving up so much contact with the church. However, as I started to spend less time involved with Christian activities, and more time with the Lord, I experienced a fresh and new relationship with God. I developed a new routine. Each time Glenn left the house to be with his friends, instead of worrying about him, I worshipped the Lord and prayed for my husband. I would pray scriptures into his life, asking that angels would guard him. It was a lovely time of intimacy with Jesus. My priority was praying for Glenn's salvation, but I also had to work on my attitude towards Glenn, and become the wife that God wanted me to be.

I discovered I Peter 3:1–7, and wrestled with this chapter,

knowing I would have to put it into practice if I were to reach out to my husband:

> **Wives, in the same way be submissive to your husbands so that, if any of them do not believe the word, they may be won over without words by the behaviour of their wives, when they see the purity and reverence of your lives. Your beauty should not come from outward adornment, such as braided hair and the wearing of gold jewellery and fine clothes. Instead, it should be that of your inner self, the unfading beauty of a gentle and quiet spirit, which is of great worth in God's sight. For this is the way the holy women of the past who put their hope in God used to make themselves beautiful. They were submissive to their own husbands, like Sarah, who obeyed Abraham and called him her master. You are her daughters if you do what is right and do not give way to fear.**

I had to choose to put this into practice, even though it was so hard to submit to a non-Christian husband.

For many years, I was a 'closet Christian' keeping my faith low key, and as non-invasive as possible at home. As I learned to submit to my husband, I noticed a softening in his attitude towards my faith. In 1995, I started attending a ladies' prayer meeting on Friday mornings, whilst Glenn was at work, and it was at this meeting that we collectively prayed for our non-Christian husbands. Someone suggested that we pray for a road to Damascus experience for Glenn. I was instantly reminded of my prayer for him many years before. So I continued to ask Jesus for a Damascus road conversion for my husband—always believing he would get one!

Glenn would occasionally come with me to Christian events, mainly to appease me. About a year before his conversion, we were invited to hear Jean Neal, who had received a miraculous healing of a spinal problem, speak at a church supper. To my amazement, Glenn accepted the invitation. Jean's testimony was powerful. We had a pleasant evening, and it passed without incident. Then, to my horror, as we were leaving, she made a beeline for us. My heart sank as I was so worried that she would upset Glenn, and I would have to live with the fallout. She looked straight into my eyes and asked if I was seeking a ministry from the Lord. I said I was, but was not free to do so because my husband was not a Christian. She turned to Glenn and asked, "What are you messing about at?" I braced myself for an explosion, but instead he grinned at her and said that he was not ready to ask Jesus into his life. The two of them chatted comfortably for some time, whilst I watched the scene unfold before me. I could not believe there was such an instant rapport between them. Glenn was obviously more than happy to answer her questions honestly. She made it quite clear to him that his time of resisting God was nearly over, and that God wanted men like him in Christian ministry. Turning to me, she said, "And you need to know that your husband is right on the edge; he will soon be a Christian." I could barely breathe. When we got home, I expected a strong reaction; amazingly his mood was relaxed and happy. God was at work!

Almost a year later, on 8th December 1997, I prepared a birthday meal for Glenn. It had not dawned on me that it was a Friday night—the evening when Glenn always went out with his friends. Somehow, that had not sunk in; I assumed he would prefer to stay at home with me.

I put a huge amount of effort into the evening, and was really looking forward to spending time with him. The house sparkled and I set the scene for a romantic evening. I dressed up, and got the children tucked up in bed early. Throughout the meal, Glenn was stony faced. He obviously had no desire to be in my company. It was like eating with an enemy, and it was agonising. I tried to make conversation and play the adoring wife, but conversation was impossible: he did not show any appreciation for my efforts. It was obvious that he wanted to be elsewhere. I felt really pushed out, and terribly hurt. All I wanted to do was show him how much I loved him and make him feel precious. His attitude towards me was indescribably painful. I went into the kitchen to make the coffee, and call out to God for his help. I was desperate for God to salvage the situation. When I returned, Glenn was ready to go out: he had his coat on and was heading for the door. So much for my prayers for help!

At this point, all my good intensions vanished. The submissive wife finally 'flipped her lid'! I cannot remember the things I said to him, but I do know that I totally lost control. He started to yell back at me, and was obviously goading me. The argument deteriorated to an all time low, and I slapped him across the face. His head jolted backwards and I started kicking him. He tried to restrain me, but I kept lashing out. Whilst I was kicking him, all I could think was, "How do I stop this? What a brilliant witness to Jesus this is!" I was in a wild frenzy, and could not stop, even though I desperately wanted to. I eventually broke free from his grip and ran upstairs. I fell on my knees and called out to God. Never before in my life had I felt so unhappy, and I was appalled by my behaviour. I remember telling God that I was so sorry for being such a poor witness to Glenn; and feeling absolutely dreadful, and so shocked, by what had happened.

I have always been such a placid person, and have never been physically violent. As I sat on the floor, weeping, I honestly believed I would never see my husband again. I could not imagine what would possess him to stay with me after my performance. My world was falling apart and I was powerless to stop it.

After some time, Glenn came into the bedroom and sat quietly on the end of the bed, with his head in his hands. I just fell down at his feet and asked him to forgive me. He responded by saying that he should never have pushed me to breaking point, and that he was so sorry. I cannot remember the rest of the evening. I know he did not go out, but it was one of the most distressing times of my life. The situation had been so horrific, I could not help but be amazed that God had stopped Glenn from leaving me. However, that night left an uneasy tension between us. We had both been shocked by our behaviour towards each other, and quietly nursed our wounds.

The week before Glenn's birthday, we had been to a church supper together. I had been desperately disappointed with the church family. As I arrived with Glenn, people sat in 'holy huddles', and Glenn and I had no one to sit with. We both felt so unwelcome, and I was concerned that it was such a poor reflection of the church. How on earth was I going to draw Glenn into church, having received such a poor reception? The battle for Glenn seemed overwhelming, and I felt I could not carry on for much longer. Little did I know that Mike Tindall had spoken to Glenn about Jesus that night, and had watered many seeds of faith. Whilst God was at work in Glenn's life, the devil was at work in mine—discouraging me.

On the night of Glen's 'road to Damascus' experience, many people sat throughout the candlelit service, specifically praying for Glenn. A great deal of prayer had been offered before God for my husband over the years; and this had intensified in recent months. There was an air of expectancy that night, and I thought about the expectancy of the shepherds on the night Jesus was born. The preaching was based on the theme of darkness and light, and people were called to get themselves right with God. I was reminded of the passage from I John, which Glenn had written in my Bible, nearly a decade earlier.

The whole family enjoyed the service, and I went home really excited. I got the children into bed, prayed for a while, and went to bed myself. I was drifting off to sleep when I became aware of an uncontrollable wailing outside our home. Someone was deeply distressed. To my horror, I realised it was Glenn. I remember asking God what had happened. I started to pray frantically. I was mortified, and was glued to the bed as I called out to God for his help. Glenn eventually bounded up the stairs, threw open the bedroom door, and blurted out between his sobs that he had given his life to Jesus. I was stunned, and it was some time before I could understand the significance of what had happened.

Eventually, I threw my arms around him, and thanked and praised God. His story was amazing. Glenn had received his Damascus road experience. God had answered my prayers. Calling Mike Tindall seemed the obvious thing to do, as I did not know how to handle the situation. Glenn was so distressed; I knew he needed to talk to another man.

The following morning, Glenn announced to the children, then aged six and nine, that he loved Jesus. The memory of Glenn's beaming, tear-stained face, as he cradled the children in his arms will stay with me for ever.

Our lives are so different now. Glenn still goes out with his friends, but that no longer makes me feel threatened or insecure. I have my husband back, and he has once again become my best friend. He is a much softer, sensitive and caring person. His passion for Jesus is wonderful to see. Every day, I thank God for answering my prayers for Glenn. My husband is such a special man, and has a lot to give. I know that the best is yet to come—for us both.

I made so many mistakes over the years. I should have been discreet about what I shared with Glenn. My enthusiasm for Jesus threatened him, and blinded me to his concerns and fears. After Glenn's conversion, I stopped praying for him in a deep and passionate way; but I now realise that was a huge mistake. I should have continued to be his spiritual support. My family commitments have changed, as the children have grown up. Naturally, as they grew into teenagers, the house became noisier and busier, so evenings were no longer quite as easy for prayer! But it is vitally important to find time to pray for the man you love.

It seems so strange now, thinking back to our life before Glenn's conversion. I know his behaviour was bad for so long, but it is hard now to find the words to describe how it was. I remember the look on his face when I mentioned Jesus, but not his words or actions. In a similar way, anyone who has had a child will know it is hard to describe labour pains. It is the same with Glenn's pre-conversion behaviour. I have forgotten the intensity of his vileness. It is as though Jesus has healed the memory. The pain that I went through for so many years now seems insignificant. I had not realised, until I read Glenn's testimony, that he thought I had given my life to Jesus after the Graham Kendrick concert. That was not the case; I had simply been blessed with the Holy Spirit that night.

If I were to offer advice to anyone, it would have to be that you should *never* give up believing that Jesus will give you the desire of your heart. 'Let go, and let God.' Pray and pray, and when you think you have prayed enough, pray some more. Hold fast to this promise:

"Believe in the Lord Jesus, and you will be saved — you and your household."

Acts 16:31

I have prayed this prayer for you:

Lord, you know how I longed for my husband to know you. You saw all my tears and heard every cry. Father, I ask that you will bless every person who reads this book with the sure knowledge that you see their tears and hear their cries. You are a faithful God, and I know you will answer their petition for their loved ones. Thank you, Father, in Jesus' name. Amen.

7

Ivan Butcher

Where can I go from your Spirit?
Where can I flee from your presence?
Psalm 139:7

I was brought up in a non-Christian household; my parents were not churchgoers, but as a child I was sent to Sunday school at the local parish church—because it was the 'nice thing to do'. After some time, my sister and I joined the 'tin tabernacle', which was a railway mission; the main reason being that they had an annual outing to the seaside and I wanted to go! They were lovely people at the Sunday school; the man who led it was an ordinary man (a Justice of the Peace). I remember being impressed with the fact that he did not wear a dog collar. I enjoyed the stories, and we had great fun.

It was at Sunday school that I developed an interest in God. I liked my own dad: we got on very well. So the father figure was a very positive one for me. From the outset, I never had any difficulty with the idea that there is a Creator: it struck me as obvious that *all this* could not have come about by chance.

In my early teens, I used to listen to Radio Luxembourg. One night there was a famine appeal. Whilst listening, I was struck with the reality that there were thousands of kids my age who would not have a tomorrow; and that hit me hard. Several things hit me simultaneously. Firstly, I knew I could not solve the problem on a personal level; my pocket money just did not stretch that far. Secondly, and most importantly, I felt with absolute conviction that Jesus was telling me: "You share the planet with those children; what I have provided for you is also provided for them." I knew this was a call from the Lord Jesus himself to follow him, and at least acknowledge I both could and should play a part that would help. I knew he would show me what part I could play. I knew I was not being called to be a missionary, or anything specific like that. It was simply to acknowledge we all share the same planet, the same finite resources; and that the same loving God looks on each of us and says, "I've given you all you need. There is enough to go round. Do it my way and it will work." The third thing was that I was absolutely scared stiff, because I could see the truth but I could not deal with it. The trouble was I saw the catch. To me, admitting that God's way was right also meant admitting that my ways needed changing, in order to come in line with his way. I saw that agreeing with God was the thin end of the wedge. If I conceded this point, how much else would I have to concede? Where would it all end? I might even end up one of those cranky, 'born again' types!

I knew that, once I had acknowledged the truth, I would also have to acknowledge a responsibility to those children, and a responsibility to Jesus. At that point I could acknowledge a responsibility to God the Father, but not yet to Jesus. I was distinctly uncomfortable with him. I knew I would have to give him my life, so that he could use me to do something about the problem. I am ashamed to say that I rejected him because it frightened me too much.

So, having rejected the call, I became adept at keeping God at arm's length. As a result, I had years of agonies, because I knew I had met with the Lord that night, rejected him; and knew I was wrong to do so. There started my wrestling match with God. It was to take twenty years before I finally gave in and allowed our loving and oh, so patient, God, to bring me, gently but irrevocably, to that re-birth I had so unnecessarily feared.

Jesus was unbelievably gentle and patient with me for many years. I did get to sleep that night, and, when I woke up the next morning, the world had not fallen apart. How many children died from famine that night, I have no idea; but I do know that there then began a process in my life which went on for two decades. At odd intervals, I would be reminded of that challenge. I knew this was not a challenge to go and be a missionary, or anything dramatic. It was simply a challenge to admit that I had a role to play in taking the love of Jesus to others. God's gentle promptings are vivid in my mind, to this day.

At that time, we lived with my paternal grandmother. My parents were licenced victuallers, having traded from the same premises for five generations. We often visited my maternal grandmother in Bury. My sister, Libby, and I would be dispatched on the coach, in the care of the bus driver. We felt terribly grown up and important. Grandma was a lovely lady; I remember her home as a loving, happy, secure place to be. She lived in a solidly built, 1930s house, with great big wooden window frames. Many times, I would wake up in the middle of the night with the silhouette of the window frame making a huge cross on the wall. Every time I woke and saw the shadow, a gentle, loving voice would always say, "*I am still here; I still want you.*" The voice was never reproachful. It was not a telling off; it was such a quiet, gentle, wooing voice; and I knew it was Jesus—urging me to see what he wanted me to be part of.

Time and time again, I rejected his voice, because I was so frightened. I was afraid that, once I said 'yes' to him, I would lose control and not be in charge of my life. I feared what he would do to me or where he would take me. I knew he would not let anything bad happen to me, but, even as a teenager, I just could not take the chance of not being in control of my life.

I knew love in full measure from my earthly parents, so

I had no problem accepting love from anyone—except from Jesus. The fact that the Lord, the Creator of the universe, saw fit to say, "I want you" was overwhelming; yet I still rejected him. Also overwhelming was the fact that Jesus chose such loving surroundings to reach out to me. Quite often, I would be out in the street and my eye would be drawn to the shape of a cross: each time, I was absolutely sure it was the Lord Jesus saying, "This is what I have done for you."

At grammar school, we had daily assembly. I enjoyed singing, and belonged to the choir, but I hated the choir practices: singing the same bar over and over again was so boring. There was a church side to my life, but it was a formal one. I gave up attending the 'tin tabernacle', as I had grown out of it. As grammar school boys, we traipsed through the town in cassocks, to the cathedral for Founders' Day services. We sang in Latin, and heard pompous diatribes from learned men in mortarboards. I had years of institutional religion, but it had lost its heart. None of it touched me like the silhouette of the cross on the bedroom wall at Grandma's house. Even though I did not want anything to do with God, I was always aware of him and loathed what I saw as religious hypocrisy. During a Founders' service, I was once assigned to place the local dignitaries on the right or left at the front of the cathedral, according to their political standing. I refused to do this, and seated the Mayor and Corporation amongst the general congregation, justifying my actions to my school masters by claiming that all men are equal before God.

My sister, Libby, shocked our family by announcing she had become a born again Christian! I could not understand why she would want to do such a thing. She became involved with a group of people (lovely people, but at the time I refused to acknowledge that) who were on fire for the Lord. She was ecstatic when Cliff Richard became a Christian; and could not wait for Billy Graham to visit town. I was horrified. I remember her coming home one night from a Christian meeting, and pronouncing judgement on Jehovah's Witnesses. I was delighted: at last, I had a reason to dismiss Christianity—I suddenly had an example of what I disliked.

I thought her irrational and judgemental. I had protracted arguments with myself, and felt at ease with the thought that there could be God the Father, but profoundly ill at ease with Jesus. The Holy Spirit just did not figure in my understanding at all.

I left school, and eventually started working as a customs officer, which was so self-evidently socially worthwhile to me. I always felt that, if I was taking drugs or pornography off the streets, I was contributing something to society. I was privileged to find my work exciting and thoroughly enjoyable. Whilst working on the drug squad, I saw the seamier side of life; the adrenaline flowed, and I enjoyed putting people away. However, I always felt conscious that I should behave honourably in the course of my duty. Yes, I would enjoy taking criminals off the streets, but I was mindful that they were fellow human beings, and deserved to be treated with dignity. My parents were hugely supportive of my role as an undercover officer, and tolerated my long haired, hippy look. I was so convincing as a 'drop out' that a police officer in Picadilly once tried to arrest me! I would often return to my parents' home with a team of tired and hungry customs officials. Mum and dad would feed and shelter us all, and often allowed us to use their car for surveillance duties. Life was full and so rewarding. I had no need of God, and continued to ignore his gentle promptings.

I eventually met Mary, my wife. She and my sister were nurses in the Queen Alexandra's Royal Naval Nursing Service; and life was complete. My sister, Libby, a committed Christian, would often try to talk to me about Jesus, but I always gave her short change. When she married, my father initially refused to go to her wedding because she wanted to marry in the Free Church that she belonged to. In his opinion it was not a proper marriage because it was not in a proper church: an interesting argument considering he was not a Christian, and certainly one she did not deserve, as she was the only member of the family who truly believed.

When Mary and I announced we were to marry in the parish church, he was hugely relieved. We both wanted to marry in the sight of God. Mary believed in God, but was very quiet about her faith. I believed in God, but did not want to get involved, especially as I was not at all sure about Jesus. We enjoyed a good marriage, and eventually had three children. Our eldest child's baptism was a simple affair. We just turned up at the church, babe in arms, and were given the words of Baptism to recite. I remember staring down at the words, thinking, "I don't believe any of this." So I muttered into my beard, and pretended to say the words, feeling distinctly uncomfortable. By the time child number two came along, I was prepared for the 'beard muttering', but my unease was even greater. By the time our third child was baptised, I had put my life right with God, so her baptism was a wonderfully joyous occasion for me. By then, we had moved to Lingfield, where the local church was very active. I can clearly see God's hand at work throughout our lives together. One of the most amazing chains of events was our move to Lingfield. We had actually agreed the sale of a three bedroom, semi-detached house in another village. We were due to sign the contracts at 2 p.m., but, a couple of hours before we were due at the solicitor's, our estate agent telephoned me to ask if I would be interested in another property. He offered us a four bedroom, detached house for the same price, providing we would agree the sale that day. We raced off to see the house, and fell in love with it. We bought the house and moved within a month, settling in quickly. Mary became interested in attending church occasionally, but I did not have any inclination to go with her. Her faith was never a big issue between us.

One particular evening, I asked Mary what she had been doing that day. Expecting the usual round of domestic answers, she shocked me by saying she had been on a Christian retreat to learn more of God. I was suddenly wide awake and we talked into the small hours. I was surprised by her commitment and passion for Jesus, and once again started to think about a creator God.

I had a small allotment and loved the idyllic setting—warm evenings, light nights, church bell practice ringing in the distant background. Robert, aged about three years, asked me, "Dad, how do you make runner beans grow?"

I absent-mindedly replied, "I don't. I just put the beans in the ground and God makes them grow."

"Who is God?" Rob asked. His question ripped through me. Suddenly, I was faced with the fact that my three-year-old child was asking me the question I had been wrestling with since I was a boy.

I did not want my son to have all the anguish I had over the years, and I certainly did not want to lie to him. As I did not know the answer to the question, I resolved to find out once and for all. At that time, the Lingfield church was running a Christian basics course called *Living in the Spirit*. It was an inter-denominational, 'come and ask questions' course, and similar to the *Alpha* course. I decided to attend, but not before I had written myself a contract. I wrote down: "I give myself permission to get up and walk out if this gets hyper emotive, hard sell, or 'glory hallelujah'. I want this to be cold and rational, and I want to be in charge."

In the first session they talked about God the Father. I felt quite comfortable, so I had no excuse not to go back the following week. There were people of different denominations all under the same roof, all talking about the love of the same God, and my objections began to crumble. I went back the second week, still very fearful. This time they talked about sinfulness—not in any heavy way, simply that none of us are what we should or could be. I could identify with that, so I still felt comfortable. Jesus had not been mentioned yet, so I had no reason to trigger my get out clause.

By the third week, they spoke of forgiveness. That was when the cross was mentioned, and that was when Jesus made sense at last. I could see where he fitted in to the argument. I went home with a great deal to think about.

During a less structured week, we sat in small horseshoe shaped groups. Each group had an empty chair. We were invited to come forward for prayer by sitting in the empty chair. Before I knew what I was doing, I was up and out of my chair. I think I was probably the first for prayer that night. It was in that single moment that I knew I had found the right time to put my life right with Jesus. So I sat on the chair, and Jesus met me. The relief I felt was enormous: I went home that night, light and free. I did not have masses of answers. In fact, I had even more questions, but I knew I had at last found where my answers would come from. That was the beginning of my walk with the Lord, and the end of my resisting him.

All those years of fighting went, and I was finally able to say, "Yes, Lord, I'm yours. I'm sorry I've been pig-headed, and maligned my sister and other Christians, and used them as an excuse to ignore you. No more, Lord, it's your agenda now, even though I'm still frightened."

I did not lose control of my life, nor did I become a religious 'weirdo'. Life carried on as usual, for a long time, whilst I learnt more about Jesus.

Mary and I committed ourselves to Jesus, and quickly became active within the church, taking Sunday school and youth sessions. We were asked to talk with a group of young people about marriage, and, following that session, we both felt our lives were about to change. I knew that I wanted to give something back to Jesus, and decided to go into the ministry. Mary did not resist; in fact, she told me that she had known for some time that I would eventually end up as a vicar. I studied at Oak Hill Theological College in London, and, shortly afterwards, was ordained in the Anglican ministry at Bristol Cathedral in 1994. I have now been a parish vicar for seven years —and what a time we have had. God had challenged us and blessed us, and I know it was the right thing to do. It has been an absolute privilege to serve the Lord.

One of the things that kept me fighting Jesus for so long was that I was frightened of being changed; but I discovered that becoming a Christian enriched my life enormously. I am always mindful of my fears and arguments, when talking to non-Christians about Jesus. I had expected to be embarrassed to my boots to be known as a Christian, but I never was. I am so frequently challenged that Jesus waited patiently twenty years for me, and I must not dare get impatient with other people. That is the nature of our loving God. It was never him not saying "come", with open arms. It was always me saying, "no", because I was frightened. I still have the same sense of humour —only better. I still have a sense of awe when I think of creation —except I now know the Creator.

It is with great joy that Mary and I are about to celebrate our silver wedding anniversary. At the time we got married, I no more expected to celebrate our twenty fifth year together as a vicar than to have cancer at the age of fifty. Yet here we are, and both are true, as is the fact that I am enjoying life immensely. Jesus' teachings strengthen me, especially the staggering truth of claims such as, **"I have come that they may have life, and have it to the full"** (John 10:10), and, **"Who of you by worrying can add a single hour to his life?"** (Matthew 6:27). These are powerful antidotes to otherwise dispiriting ill-health, and have released me to put my energies into enjoying the present moment, and leaving the future in God's trustworthy hands. My physical body is sick. I do not know whether Jesus will heal me or call me home. but I do not mind, because he knows what is best for me, and that is good enough for me. Jesus is life blood and oxygen to me, and I know he will be for eternity.

The essential thing for all of us is to put God where he belongs—at the centre of our lives. Make plans, dream dreams, hold onto hopes, by all means. You were created to do so. But acknowledge, too, that you and I do not have the power to make them come to fruition; for that we need to turn to God. Then, having turned to him, we must leave it up to him, how and when he will deal with us. Our part is to go on with life, thanking God for all his blessings; and trusting that he truly knows what is best, and can give us what is ultimately for our good.

If you knew that this month were your last, would you use the time any differently? And what if the certainty was there, but the timescale shorter or longer? Would a final year be any different from a final day or hour? The day must come to us all; so, too, the hour, the minute, the final breath. For all who listen and respond to the call of our heavenly Father, the final day on this earth is the one when we move on to the greatest hope and promise of all: eternal life through Jesus Christ.

"For I know the plans I have for you," declares the Lord, "plans to prosper you and not to harm you, plans to give you hope and a future."

Jeremiah 29:11

Life on earth is transient. My hope and future lies with the Creator of heaven and earth, and it is to him I give thanks for a praying wife—a wife without whom I could not have dared to respond to God's call on my life.

8

Mary Butcher

I joined the Queen Alexandra's Royal Naval Nursing Service at eighteen years of age, and started my nurse training. Then, for the first time in my life, I was faced with death. As I began to think about what happened to people when they died, I set out on a road which would lead me to become a Christian; though I was not, at that time, born again.

I started to learn more about God through the Navy Christian Fellowship, was confirmed as an adult, and attended church regularly. My faith was quiet, though very important to me. I became friends with Libby, who eventually introduced me to her brother, Ivan. She and Ivan were very close as children, but her conversion to Christianity was a huge shock to him. He was never antagonistic towards Libby, simply complacent. He seemed content not to have religion in his life.

At first, we got on very well as platonic friends; we were both busy with our careers, and were content to be part of a group of friends. Then I was posted to London, recruiting nurses into the navy, and as Ivan lived nearby I would occasionally call him up and ask him to escort me to various functions. He was such an uncomplicated, transparent person and we became great friends. Over the years our friendship strengthened—so much so that, without realising it, we had fallen in love.

Then came a posting abroad to Malta and, before I left, Ivan shocked me by asking me to marry him. In those days, married women were not allowed to serve in the forces. Ironically, part of my job was to discourage nurses from marrying and leaving the profession. The force was losing too many experienced nurses, and needed to hold on to them. I was about to become another such statistic! We married in church, as we both felt it was the right thing to do; as I believed in God, I never considered marrying anywhere else.

After our marriage, my awareness of God mellowed into the background, because Ivan was not interested and we were both very busy. I stopped going to church, and became thoroughly involved in Ivan's life and my work as a civilian midwife. I did not feel uncomfortable about marrying a non-Christian, as no one in my church ever mentioned it to us. Ivan was a good man, and I resigned myself to waiting for him.

Throughout our marriage, I prayed regularly for him to know God; but it was never a big, dramatic issue for us. We simply got on with life peacefully. Ivan's sister and husband prayed regularly for Ivan for many years, but it was not a frantic pressure. As I recall that time, Psalm 131 holds a very special place in my heart:

My heart is not proud, O LORD,
my eyes are not haughty;
I do not concern myself with great matters
or things too wonderful for me.
But I have stilled and quietened my soul;
like a weaned child with its mother,
like a weaned child is my soul within me.
O Israel, put your hope in the LORD
both now and for evermore.

After we had our children and moved to Lingfield, I felt a real hunger to get back into a church, and I started attending a ladies' weekly Christian group. My faith was quietly rekindled. It was a time of spiritual growth for me, and it was here that I asked Jesus into my life and became a 'born again' Christian. I did not know how to tell Ivan what was happening to me. Thankfully, Jesus helped me out. One evening, after attending a Christian retreat, he just happened to ask me what I had been doing, and I had to be honest, own up, and tell him where I had been. He was genuinely interested in my relationship with Jesus, and was full of questions. We talked about my faith until the early hours of the morning.

In Lingfield we became great friends with The Reverend Alan Ramsay, who had a profound influence on both our lives. He patiently taught us both more of the love of Jesus, and gave us wise counsel. He quickly recognised Ivan's genuine love for God, and his leadership qualities, and drew us into the church. Eventually, Ivan faced a dilemma regarding a promotion within Customs and Excise, and Alan told him not to worry, as he would not be in Customs for much longer: he felt that we would be called into full time ministry. I agreed with Alan, as I had had the same feeling for a long time. Not long after that, Ivan decided to go to theological college and become an ordained minister in the Church of England.

Ivan loved his work as a customs officer, and it was a huge sacrifice for him to leave; but God has really blessed us over the years. Life as a vicar's wife has been different. Very quickly, I had to learn to share my husband with a lot of other people, but the life and work has brought us great friendships and blessings. Ivan loved the church, and his early death has been a great blow to us all.

The one thing I am sure of is that God's hand continues to be on our family. He is just and faithful, and always honours our call for help. Numerous prayers have been answered, and I am on the receiving end of his love for me continuously.

I do not know why Ivan went to be with the Lord so young, but I know with absolute assurance that he is in heaven. I am so grateful to God for allowing me to have shared my life with such an honourable and godly man.

Author's Note:

When I told Ivan that I wanted to write this book, he was immediately fired with enthusiasm and agreed to tell me about his journey of faith; as always, he wanted to honour God. Ivan was undergoing treatment for aggressive prostatic cancer. At that time none of us anticipated his rapid decline, nor did we know he had such a short time to live.

On the day of our final interview, Ivan was walking with the aid of two walking sticks. His pelvic bone had started to crumble, and mobility was difficult and clearly painful. Whilst we chatted, I recorded our conversation on a tape recorder. We prayed before we started talking. I asked the Lord to inspire Ivan's words in order to touch the lives of his readers. Ivan, in turn, prayed for a rich harvest from this book. Throughout our chat, he was oblivious to his physical state. In fact, the more he spoke of Jesus, the more animated he became. Although Ivan was a very bright and intelligent man, he became almost boyish when he spoke of his love for the Lord; his enthusiasm was contagious.

I mentioned to Ivan that I was thrilled to see that, despite his obvious discomfort, he still had a twinkle in his eye when he spoke of Jesus. He looked at me, grinned broadly, and said, "Oh Lynn, talking about Jesus is life blood and oxygen to me." I was so conscious, that afternoon, that a miracle was unfolding before my eyes.

We can all praise God when things are going well for us, but to praise and trust him in the midst of disastrous circumstances is a real test of faith. Here was a man in the prime of his life whose body was being ravaged by cancer, yet he continued to honour and delight in Jesus. "I don't know whether the Lord will cure me or whether he wants me to die well, but

I don't mind because, either way, it's in his hands." Ivan told me that, given a choice in the matter, he would prefer to live, simply because he loved his family and felt that there was so much more work to do in the church. However, he was content to continue to trust the Lord —because God had not got it wrong so far. As a nurse, I have cared for many terminally ill people, but none like Ivan. Throughout his illness, he never doubted that God knew what was best; he bore his sickness with grace. Whilst Ivan was bedridden, he and his family worshipped God, read psalms and prayed, with just as much enthusiasm as if he were in his parish church. He died as he lived, surrounded by those he loved, and trusting in God for his and their future.

His thanksgiving service was held on 11th September, 2001, at 2 p.m. Following the service, we learned of the dreadful atrocity which had taken place in New York on that day. Someone said to me afterwards that, had we known about the tragedy, we probably would not have gone ahead with the service. My response to that was to recall that all of us will remember where we were and what we were doing on that day. I am so thankful to God that I was giving thanks to Jesus for a man who lived for, and loved, Jesus. I thank God that I was praising Jesus, and reading the words of Psalm 139 to a packed church—words which are significant for all those who live with the consequences of that tragic day. Ivan loved Psalm 139, meditating on it throughout his illness. Four days before he died, we read it, and prayed together.

O LORD, you have searched me
and you know me.
You know when I sit and when I rise;
you perceive my thoughts from afar.
You discern my going out and my lying down;
you are familiar with all my ways.
Before a word is on my tongue
you know it completely, O LORD.

You hem me in—behind and before;
  you have laid your hand upon me.
Such knowledge is too wonderful for me,
    too lofty for me to attain.

Where can I go from your Spirit?
Where can I flee from your presence?
If I go up to the heavens, you are there;
if I make my bed in the depths, you are there.
    If I rise on the wings of the dawn,
    if I settle on the far side of the sea,
  even there your hand will guide me,
    your right hand will hold me fast.

If I say, "Surely the darkness will hide me
  and the light become night around me,"
even the darkness will not be dark to you;
    the night will shine like the day,
    for darkness is as light to you.

For you created my inmost being;
  you knit me together in my mother's womb.
I praise you because I am fearfully and wonderfully
              made;
      your works are wonderful,
        I know that full well.
  My frame was not hidden from you
    when I was made in the secret place.
When I was woven together in the depths of the earth,
    your eyes saw my unformed body.
    All the days ordained for me
      were written in your book
    before one of them came to be.

How precious to me are your thoughts, O God!
    How vast is the sum of them!
      Were I to count them,
  they would outnumber the grains of sand.

When I awake, I am still with you.
If only you would slay the wicked, O God!
Away from me, you bloodthirsty men!
They speak of you with evil intent;
your adversaries misuse your name.
Do I not hate those who hate you, O LORD,
and abhor those who rise up against you?
I have nothing but hatred for them;
I count them my enemies.

Search me, O God, and know my heart;
test me and know my anxious thoughts.
See if there is any offensive way in me,
and lead me in the way everlasting.

I asked Ivan if there was anything he wanted to pray about. He gave a great big grin, lowered his voice, as if we were about to share some great secret, and said, "Lynn, Jesus knows everything. He's been here all the time." The joy in his voice was unmistakable, and his faith thrilled me beyond words. To his dying day, Ivan remained sure in the knowledge that God would only do what was best for his life. Ivan touched many lives. Some of those contacts were lasting, some fleeting, but one thing is true: he really was a man of God. Psalm 139 blessed Ivan through years of ministry, as well as in the long days and nights of physical and emotional pain. The words blessed him, just as they have blessed others through the centuries. May you too be blessed. Ivan wrote this, shortly before he went to be with the Lord:

Why this,
Why me,
Why now
Why not?

I praise you Lord, that you are all I need;
And though I know I am not all I should be,

Your love will intercede,
And bring redemption for my years
Misspent in vain rebellion against your love.
It was for me that you shed tears
As o'er Jerusalem your heart was moved.
"You look for peace," you cried to them,
And they, with closed eyes, failed peace to see.
My heart goes to Jerusalem
For in their blindness I see shades of me.
Yet, Praise You! For your love won through
And claim'd my heart — which now belongs to you.
So how should I doubt you, who are my friend;
My Saviour, Lord, Redeemer without end.

Ivan was a super vicar; he loved the Lord, and it was a joy to share fellowship with him. He is missed dreadfully, but we are comforted to know that he is spending eternity in heaven. We will meet again one day; this parting is for a short time. We are blessed to have known him and shared our lives with him.

Thank you to my dear friend Mary Butcher, for allowing me to continue to write about Ivan.

L.F.

9

Mick Maddocks

Working as a lorry driver for most of my life has meant that I have been used to spending many hours on my own, with no one to talk to, apart from the occasional hitchhiker. I have always believed in God, and, on those long journeys, would often talk to him. Our conversations were very one-sided, as I never heard back from him, though! Whilst I was aware of God, I did not *know* him. I did not think of God as an 'old man with a long white beard', but as a mighty spiritual being; I simply had a sense of someone—or something—much bigger than myself.

I considered myself a Christian because, in childhood, my parents had told me I should say, if asked, that I belonged to the Church of England. God was never mentioned in our home, and we never went to church, except for the standard weddings, christenings and funerals; and I do not remember many of those. It was always accepted that, because we were not bad people, that made us Christians; and whatever heaven was, we were all confident we would go there when we died. Janice and I married in church, but only because it was the social convention in those days. Church weddings always seemed much 'nicer' than those which took place in register offices. Janice was not religious, although, as a little girl, she had attended a Baptist Sunday school. She grew out of religion and stopped going to church by her teens. She and our daughter, Nichola, were always looking for answers, and trying to see what lay in the future: they were addicted to horoscopes, and tarot card readings. I was not interested: it seemed to me to be all a load of 'mumbo jumbo'. We never talked about God, and we went to church only when we had to, for weddings, funerals and christenings.

Quite out of the blue, I was made redundant from my driving job and, as I had spent all my life working with lorries and cars, I set up a motor repair business with a friend. We were quite successful and I, like many men, fell into the trap of investing most of my time in my business. Consequently, as a family we went separate ways, and lived separate lives. I spent all my time in the garage, and Janice and Nichola did their own 'mother and daughter' thing. I was a typical working class bloke. I enjoyed a couple of pints occasionally, smoked thirty cigarettes a day, and swore a fair bit. I worked hard, enjoyed my role as breadwinner, and was quite content with my life. I was happily married to Janice, and thoroughly enjoyed being a father. What more could a man need?

My relationship with Nichola deteriorated when she approached her teen years. She understandably rebelled against my heavy handedness, and our relationship was very poor. We hardly spoke, unless we were rowing about something. There was constant friction between us, and Janice was caught in the middle—forever the peacekeeper. I was so scared my little girl would go off the rails that I ruled her with an iron rod. We did not talk much, and I relied on Janice to keep track of Nicola's activities. We kept her on a tight rein, mindful that the teenage years were fraught with dangers.

Things worsened when Nichola went on a school trip to Germany at the age of thirteen. Whilst she was away, she had enormous freedom; she was allowed to visit bars, stay up late and, basically, suit herself. When she returned home, she was withdrawn and anti-social. I was desperate to know how to stop her going off the rails and how to reach out to her. As our relationship had deteriorated so much, we had little to draw on, and the situation continued to deteriorate. She longed for the freedom and lifestyle she had enjoyed in Germany, and I wanted her to do as she was told; the friction between us escalated. The tension at home was unbearable, and I found myself devoting more and more time to my business—not just out of necessity, but also as a form of escape.

This situation continued for another two years. The atmosphere at home was tense, and my relationship with my daughter was seemingly hopeless. When Nichola was fifteen years old, her friend invited her to join her family on a Christian holiday. Nichola knew the mum was a Christian, but like Nichola her friend was not interested in religion, so she felt secure in the knowledge that she had an ally, and would just go for a laugh. Nichola was only too pleased to get away from home, and went off on holiday with her friends, oblivious to the fact that her life would never be the same again. Neither would ours.

When Nichola returned home, I was the one that greeted her on the doorstep. She said, "Hello, dad. I've been saved."

I flippantly replied, "Oh yes, what from?" She came inside and gave us both a huge hug. We were stunned by her display of physical emotion; we were not a very tactile family at the best of times. Having spent the last two years at loggerheads with Nichola, the last thing I expected was a hug from her. Whilst I was still reeling from the hug, she reiterated that she had become a Christian. I said, "Great; I'm a Christian."

She looked directly at me, and calmly said, "No, you're not, dad. You have to have Jesus in your life to be a Christian." Although I was completely shocked by her words and her confidence, I was determined not to let my teenage daughter see what effect her words had on me. I had been brought up to believe that I was a Christian because I believed in the existence of God. No one had told me that Jesus was part of the package. Nichola's words challenged me, and I kept turning them over in my mind. When she said, "I have become a Christian", I did not understand what she meant. How could she have become a Christian, when she had been brought up in a Christian country in the Church of England, and had been christened as a baby? To my mind, she was already a Christian. Those three words, "I have become..." haunted me continuously.

From the moment she came home, I watched Nichola change for the better. She was transformed from an uncommunicative, truculent teenager, to a sociable, friendly, loving girl. Now she started to help her mum around the house, and was extremely good company. The sullen, rebellious teenager had gone, and we were left with a delightful, confident young girl. The fact that she was absolutely besotted with Jesus was something I would have to learn to accept; if that was the price to pay, then I would accept that. She started attending church regularly, developing a strong bond with new Christian friends.

Nichola frequently invited me to church with her, and I would always give the same reply: "Church might be all right for you, Nichola, but it's not for me." I found it strange that she never argued with me, but I know now that she had discovered a far more effective weapon than arguing. She simply asked all her friends to pray for me. I was completely oblivious to the fact that my life was constantly bombarded by prayer. I did not stand a chance! As Nichola was too young to drive, I was often 'number one taxi driver'. I would take Nichola to church on a Sunday night, and then hover outside, hoping to get some idea of what they were getting up to in there. I was curious, and wanted to know what they were doing to bring about such an amazing change in my teenage daughter. Each week, someone would invite me in, but I would say, "No, no; I'll pick her up later", and would disappear at high speed, as if I were frightened of catching something. Nichola was so committed to her faith; not only did she attend church regularly, but she would also go to early morning prayer meetings and youth groups. Her lifestyle and behaviour were totally transformed. Without my realising it, my own life was undergoing a transformation, too.

I was happy that Nichola was with people I knew would

look after her. She was happy, and I could not deny the change in her, but, for some reason, I could not resist goading her at times. Even though I benefited hugely by her transformation, I could not stand the Christian music she played, and would become very irritated to see her Bible in the sitting room. I would ask her to put it away in her bedroom, as I disliked seeing it, and did not want it around the house; I found its presence offensive. I remember having a very heated conversation with Nichola, about God, and I yelled at her, "There's only one god in this house, and that's me." I remember the crushed look on Nichola's face, but I had no idea how much I was offending and hurting her. Despite my regular verbal assaults, though, she never wavered in her faith. Life settled down, and I was resigned to letting her get on with church; as long as she did not expect Janice or myself to join in, I was happy. I often asked Janice what was happening to Nichola, expecting her to be as irritated as I was. But she would just tell me to leave her alone, to let her get on with her life.

Without my being aware of it, God was already at work in Janice. Nichola would talk to her about the people in church and, like me, she was curious about the goings on there. She found herself drawn to all things religious, and would watch anything on television to do with Christianity, whilst I was out of the house. When Nichola left her Bible around, Janice would read it alone, in secret. Some time later, she told me how amazed she had been to discover that the Bible made sense. As a child, she had been introduced to the King James Version of the Bible, and did not understand the old language. But the modern version, which Nichola used, brought the word of God to life. Whilst my irritation grew, Janice was discovering that the seeds of faith sown in her childhood were coming to fruition.

One Sunday morning, whilst I was at work, Jan watched a programme called *This is the Day*, which included the verse: **"You did not choose me, but I chose you."** She was shocked by the words, and they stayed with her, just as Nichola's words, 'I have become a Christian', had stayed with me. The following Sunday, she watched another televised church service whilst doing the ironing. All the familiar things she had learnt as a child came flooding back to her, and she found herself on her knees, in floods of tears. She told the Lord she was sorry that she had rejected Jesus, and had not lived her life as he had wanted her to. In that moment she knew that she had to live a different life from then on, and follow Jesus. Right there and then, in front of the television, Janice gave her life to the Lord; but she did not say a word to me. It was hers and Nichola's little secret for a few more weeks, until the Lord had finished his work in me.

From that moment, Nichola and Janice would talk about Christianity, and pray for me. I did not have a clue what was going on. Both my daughter and wife were ganging up on me in prayer. Janice would go into our bedroom, read a psalm, and cry—because she thought that going Jesus' way would destroy our marriage. As much as she loved me, she knew she could not give up on Jesus for the second time in her life. She had to trust that he would change me. She made a conscious decision to keep quiet about her faith until the right time. She and Nichola fellowshipped in secret, and were very discreet; as I was totally oblivious to what they were doing. I was still absorbed in my business, so they had plenty of time to nurture Janice's faith and bombard heaven with prayers for my salvation.

One day, Nichola came home and announced that there was a gospel concert at her church, then invited me along. I remember thinking, 'Oh, no; here we go again.' I gave her my usual 'death stare' and said, "Look, it's okay for you, but I don't want to go."

To my surprise, a little voice from the corner of the room said, "I'd like to go." I could not believe my ears. Janice wanted to go to a gospel concert. I did not want to be left out, and felt confident that there was safety in numbers. If Jan was going, then I would be alright.

So it was that we went along to the Talbot Street Christian Centre in Nottingham—and I could not believe my eyes. About seven hundred people had given up a Saturday night to go to church! I was bowled over by the singing and preaching. I had never previously experienced anything so passionate or sincere in a church. The whole evening was amazing, and the following week I could not stop thinking about the words of the songs and the atmosphere within the church. I wanted to know what was going on, and could not fight my curiosity any longer, so I decided to attend church regularly. From that day forward, we went to church each Sunday—but only on a fact finding exercise. After each service I had plenty to say for myself, and gave everyone around me a hard time.

Unbeknown to me, God was working overtime in my spirit. I had a lot of unlearning to do. It was not a very peaceful journey for me, as every time I came out of church I was really angry. Church, to me, had meant a handful of old ladies singing two hundred year-old hymns. But these services were different: they were vibrant, warm and loving; and the people seemed so sincere. I found the preaching dynamic; I had never heard anything like it, and the message frequently disturbed me. I would come out of church and, all the way home, I would argue about the sermon with Nichola. She would answer me confidently, absolutely clear what the Bible said about the issues; she was unshakable in her stance. Janice was very quiet after each service, never rising to the bait. I interpreted her silence as agreement with me; wrong again!

A few weeks later, Nichola announced she wanted to be baptised. I could not for the life of me understand why she felt the need, as she had been christened as a baby. I thought that infant baptism was a guarantee for life. Being 'done' again as an adult was beyond me. However, she was insistent that she wanted to go through a believer's baptism, so we agreed to go and support her. First we went as usual to the earlier, morning service, and I recall that, in the course of it, the preacher gave altar calls for anyone who wanted to ask the Lord Jesus into their lives to put their hand up. To my amazement, Janice put her hand up to make a commitment, and I said, "What have you done that for? Put your hand down."

She replied, "I can't! I have got to do this." I tried to persuade her to put her hand down, but she was determined to make a commitment to Jesus. I immediately felt overwhelmed by frustration. I felt as if I were losing control of my family. I could not understand what was happening—first to my daughter and now to my wife. I stared at her, and tried to make sense of the situation. Why couldn't she put her hand down? I was extremely aware that people around were watching us.

The next thing I knew, she was being called out to the front to acknowledge her commitment to Jesus. People started streaming out to the front and Janice followed.

Whilst I was struggling to make sense of what was happening, the preacher looked at me and said, "You can come too, Mick. We've been praying for you all week."

Because I was so stunned by Janice's actions, and did not want to make a scene, I followed everyone else into a little side room. We were ushered towards individual tables and met by Christian counsellors, who welcomed everyone into God's family. The guy that got me drew the short straw. He brightly congratulated me on my decision to ask the Lord into my life, and asked if I understood what I had done by saying the prayer of commitment. Boy, did I give him a tough time. I told him, in no uncertain terms, that I had not given my heart to Jesus. So, naturally, he asked why I had gone forward. I told him that it was because the preacher had told me to, and I wanted to see what my wife was getting up to, as well. The poor man did not stand a chance: I harangued him and Jesus, and then left, in a ferocious mood.

I could not believe what Janice had done; things had gone too far, and I had to put a stop to this nonsense. I went home in a vile state of mind, and gave her and Nichola a tough time. As I had promised Nichola that I would go to her baptism, we returned to the church that evening. I was still fuming, and nonplussed by Janice's wanting to become a Christian, but I decided to grin and bear it until I could put a stop to all this religious nonsense. Before the actual baptism ceremony, Nichola, along with several other people, gave her personal testimony in front of the whole church. Once again, I was bowled over by the transformation in my daughter; her sincerity touched my heart, and I knew God was hot on my tail. It was during that service that the Lord really touched me; but it would be another three weeks before I finally gave in to him. For those three weeks, I raged against myself and against God. I was so angry all the time. I told myself that I did not need God; yet something inside me was searching frantically for him. One night, during an evening service in church, I finally decided to stop fighting. I asked the Lord Jesus to forgive me for doubting who he was, and asked him into my life. There were no flashes of lightning, nor angelic choirs —simply a feeling that I had done the right thing, at last.

Throughout my life I had been such a hard man, and the Lord really worked on my spirit. After asking him into my life, I could not stop crying: I wept buckets of tears. Everything I did seemed to induce a tearful response. It was so out of character, yet I knew it was an essential part of God clearing out the rubbish in my life. Eventually, he finished sorting out my hard heart, and almost instantly there was a dramatic change in my life —as a result of asking Jesus to take control. Now I loved talking about Jesus, and shocked my family, friends and customers by talking about the Lord incessantly. My transformation was particularly difficult for a business partner, who asked me to stop talking to him and the customers about religion—but I could not help myself. I needed to let people know what they were missing. I played Christian music in the garage as I worked, and this undoubtedly caused some embarrassment to others! I soaked up as much about God as I could; after all, I had a lifetime to make up for. I attended every church meeting I could, and found that I wanted to share Jesus with people; talking about him now came so naturally to me. Janice and I joined Nichola's church, becoming members of a large body of Spirit filled, Bible-believing Christians. We were so blessed to be embraced by some wonderful people, who patiently taught us about the Lord, and the life we were to lead. The teaching we received, both in church and from our Christian friends, was excellent; and I soon started to 're-educate' myself. At long last, I understood how I had been deceived all those years into thinking I was a Christian. I soon found an outlet for my enthusiasm and passion for Jesus, and started working with a group engaged in teen evangelism. With my experience of Nichola, I knew how not to relate to the youngsters, and God used me to reach out to those who were desperately in need of his touch.

God delivered me from a hard heart and, miraculously, from smoking, too. I accepted a cigarette from someone one day and, as I drew it, I found the taste repugnant. Suddenly, I remembered that someone had prayed for me the day before, that I would be released from smoking. I looked at the cigarettes, remembered the prayer, and knew that God was at work. From that moment, I never smoked again. I really believe that the Lord answered my prayer, and took away my desire to smoke.

Six months after I became a Christian, I felt the Lord challenge me. I knew he wanted me to give up my business. I did not know how to extricate myself from our partnership, so simply asked the Lord to sort it out. I did not say a word to Janice, nor to anyone else. I just knew God would make it quite clear to me that he was at work. On Easter Monday, at eight o'clock in the morning, my partner rang me up and offered to buy me out. I immediately agreed, as I knew that God was at work. I was aware that I had to honour God. The decision was a clear one for me: I did not even have to take time to consider the offer. I was unemployed for a few weeks, then got a job as a driver, with a large department store in Nottingham. The interview process was really rigorous. One of the first questions the interviewer asked me was, "Why did your partnership fail?" I explained that it had not failed but was very successful, yet God had called me out; and I was able to say why God had asked me to give up the business. I thought that the interviewers would think I was mad, but I felt peaceful, and I heard God speak for the first time. He told me, "Michael, this job is yours." And it was.

Since I became a believer, our family has been trans-formed. We have become much more tactile, and nothing gives me greater pleasure than to hug my daughter. I owe her a lot. We really do communicate, and are far more honest and open than we used to be. I have a much softer, compassion-ate and tolerant nature now. I am still very much a 'man's man', but instead of misusing my authority by yelling and being a hard man, I use my gifts to lead within the church. I will be eternally grateful to the Lord for blessing me with not one but two women who begged God for my salvation. My wife is an amazing woman of God, who prayed faithfully for me to share her love of God. She and Nichola made a formi-dable duo; I did not stand a chance.

I am now a church deacon; we lead a home group, and are prayer co-ordinators in a small village church. It is very dif-ferent from the powerful city church where we started our Christian life, but we are content where we are now, and richly blessed.

God constantly opens doors and brings into my life peo-ple who are desperately in need of him. For instance, we had a prophecy in our house group, that the Lord would use us. When we got home, the telephone was ringing. A man I had not heard from for over twenty two years was calling, to say he was about to have major heart surgery, and just felt the need to talk to me. He had suddenly had the urge to contact me, so he traced me through a mutual friend. I immediately visited him, and had the opportunity to pray with him. There is no doubt in my mind that God arranged that telephone call. When we met, he said, "Look at me, Mick. I'm fifty one years old and worn out; look at you, you look great." I was able to tell him about the difference Jesus had made to my life. He had known me as a smoking, swearing, drinking, 'hard man', and found a very different person from the one he had known.

I trust totally in the Lord. He knows what is best for me, and it is my greatest pleasure to honour him. There are two people in the Bible that are especially close to my heart. One is Zechariah, and the other is Mary, the mother of Jesus. The angel Gabriel told Zechariah that his wife, Elizabeth, would have a child, even though she was an old woman. Zechariah immediately doubted the angel, and said, **"How can I be sure of this?"**

The angel replied, **"I am Gabriel. I stand in the presence of God, and I have been sent to speak to you and to tell you this good news."** Because Zechariah doubted the angel's word, he was struck dumb until his son, John, was born. In contrast, when Mary was told she would have a son, she immediately accepted what the angel said to her: she did not argue. Mary and Zechariah responded differently to God's will, but God's purpose was fulfilled. The point I want to make is that whatever God has planned for you will happen. It does not matter how much you doubt or object: it will happen. He only wants what is good for us. That includes saving husbands.

I have some relatives who are not saved, as yet. But, just as my wife and daughter pleaded for my salvation, and God answered their prayers, I have pleaded for the salvation of my extended family. Knowing as I do, without a shadow of doubt, that God is faithful, I am confident he will answer my prayers for each and every one of them.

10

Nichola Maddocks

As a teenager I was not a very nice person, especially to my
dad. I went through the normal teenage emotions, whilst trying to gain my independence. As an only child, I found my
dad over protective. We clashed terribly, and we had some
dreadful, heated arguments. I was pulling one way and he
was pulling the other. I realise now that was because he
wanted to protect me, but I really could not see it at the time.
I thought he wanted to control me, and because of my frustration I lashed out. I am ashamed to say I was often physically
violent towards dad. He did not seem to trust me, nor to believe a word of what I said to him. I felt that things would
often happen which were beyond my control. I remember, on
one occasion, dad telling me to be home for a certain time
and, whilst I was out, I dropped my watch and it broke. I returned home late, but dad did not believe the broken watch
story. It was almost as if he thought I had broken the watch
deliberately, to back up a lame excuse. As a result, we did not
talk at all: we simply yelled at each other, hurling abuse and
misunderstandings. He appeared to be a very hard man, and
we failed to connect in any way. We were not a tactile family,
and did not communicate our deep feelings for each other at

all. My relationship with mum was much better, but still had room for loads of improvement. Most of our conversations revolved around my arguments with dad. It is fair to say that I was rebellious and never did a stroke of work around the house. I am ashamed to say that I felt it was mum's job, not mine.

I had a friend whose family had been Jehovah's Witnesses, but whose mother suddenly became a born again Christian, and announced she wanted to go to the Peterborough Bible week. She convinced us that there would be loads of activities for bored teenagers. I was only too glad of a week away from dad, so we agreed to go. Mum and dad were happy for me to go, as they knew the family well, and trusted I would be well looked after.

When we arrived, we had no intention of having anything to do with religious things. For the first couple of days we were absolute rebels. We poked fun at people, and played our non-Christian music as loudly as we could, to annoy the neighbours. We deliberately flirted with the boys, and were generally disruptive and rude; we were awful. I am not quite sure how it happened, but somehow we ended up at a Christian meeting. We probably thought it would be a laugh. We sat high up, right at the back of the big tent. I cannot really remember what the preacher was talking about, but I do remember at one point he mentioned insecurities in our lives. Then he had my full attention. I do not know why, but I suddenly realised that I felt overwhelmingly insecure, and had done so for some time. I knew that my parents loved me, and had given me a good home and upbringing, but his words identified something lacking in my life which was unconnected with my upbringing. I suddenly made the connection, and I realised that we all have a 'God-shaped hole' in our lives, which only God can fill. Immediately, everything seemed so clear to me. I had no control over the fact that his words pierced my heart; and I had absolutely no control over my response. He called people forward to receive Christ into their lives, and I remember saying to my friend, "I've got to go to the front." By the time I reached the platform, I was an absolute mess; tears were streaming down my face, and I was a complete wreck. I could not stop crying; I found myself in a crowd of people, praying. I fell on my knees, and asked the Lord into my life. My conversion was very emotional but very real. I knew that I had met with the Lord Jesus. For the next four days I soaked up my new commitment. The more I learnt about the Lord, the more he melted my rebellious teenage heart. My friend's mother bought me a Bible, and I attended every meeting I could. I felt as if I was at a banquet on a feeding frenzy—it was absolutely amazing. The difference was that I did not feel gorged: there was so much more room for second helpings. I could not believe what was happening to me; it was fantastic. I had no doubt that I had met with the Lord Jesus, and I had been saved. I knew who I was and where I was going. I also knew, with all my heart, that my parents were not saved. The moment that fact dawned on me, a passion and courage sprang up in me to pray for my mum and dad.

Every time I thought about my parents, I had a physical ache in my chest, which prompted me to pray for them. I constantly called out to God, and would remind him to save my parents. I prayed morning, noon and night; they were constantly on my heart, and I interceded for them non-stop. I joined a prayer triplet with friends, and we always pleaded for them before God. I asked everyone I knew to pray for my mum and dad. I also went to the leader of our church, and said to him, "I see you as my spiritual father; you're the top man, you're the boss of this church: I need your help." I told him my dad was not a Christian, and I wanted him to pray for him. He must have told the church elders, because they all prayed for dad, which I believe was a significant factor in his speedy conversion.

At times, I felt I was really hurting my parents by telling them they were not Christians, but I could not stop sharing the gospel. I was desperate for them to see the truth. Dad's reaction to my words was so painful; he constantly blasphemed, but I became even more determined to get God to change his heart. I was only fifteen at the time, but I had amazing clarity about who God was. I was a Bible-believing Christian, and my Bible said that God could do all things: that included saving my mum and dad!

Like my mother I was very aware that spiritual things were real. Before I became a Christian, I had dabbled in all sorts of things like tarot and horoscopes, so I knew there was a spiritual dimension to life. Now, as a new Christian, I knew that there was a battle on for dad, because he was not where he should be with God. I could see it so clearly by his language, actions and comments. Now I enjoyed excellent teaching, and training in discipleship, which supported my prayer determination. The more I grew in my faith, the more I prayed for dad. God was amazing, and always gave me the words to say to dad. I was still only fifteen years old, and my dad was a hard man, yet everything I said had an impact on him. There was no doubt that Jesus was in charge, and protecting me. When mum asked the Lord into her life, I knew dad would not be far behind. I am thankful to the Lord that I did not have to wait too long, because the process was so intense I was exhausted; it is a good job I had youth on my side. Seeing my dad come to the Lord has to be one of the most amazing events of my life: it was an awesome privilege to be used by the Lord in such a way. I cannot encourage people enough to not give up. Keep on praying, and get as many people as you can to pray—because it works!

11

Janice Maddocks

My testimony is quite short. I did not have to wait very long for Mick to come to faith—only three months, which is just as well, because I really do not think I could have coped with the strain for any longer than that. Like Mick, I had always considered myself a Christian, and was shocked to the core when Nichola told me I would not go to heaven because I did not have Jesus in my life. It was not just her words that struck a chord; it was her absolute conviction that she was right. She did not pull any punches, and I remember being horrified. When I protested that I was a believer at heart, she told me I was not a Christian because I was not like the other women in church. She said she could see a marked difference between their lives and mine: I just did not have Jesus in my life, therefore I was not a Christian. I felt so shocked and hurt that she compared me to other women, and found me lacking. Her words and change in behaviour had a dramatic effect on me. Following her conversion, she became helpful and caring towards both Mick and myself. Seemingly overnight, she had matured, and now seemed wise beyond her years. I could see that something supernatural had taken place in her life, and I was curious to know more. Nichola worked away at me behind the scenes, but really my journey was not too difficult, because I had met with Jesus as a little girl; and, to me, renewing my faith was like coming home. I remember watching a Christian service on television in which a verse read was, **"You did not choose me, but I chose you."** I knew, in that moment, that Jesus had waited nearly thirty years for me to acknowledge him. Having accepted Jesus into my heart, I gladly accepted the role of chief prayer warrior for my husband.

Mick was so anti-Christian that I decided not to tell him I was a believer. I was frightened of declaring my faith, because I thought I would lose Mick if he knew I was a Christian. I knew the time was not right to tell him. It was an awfully stressful time, but I knew that I could not reject Jesus for the second time in my life.

Not only did I have to keep my faith a secret, but I also had to keep my very active prayer life a secret, too. When Mick was out of the house, I would fall on my knees and call out to God to save him. I constantly read the psalms, and called on God to work a miracle in Mick's life. I interceded for him, day and night. Between us, Nichola and I put in hours of prayer for him, and we soon saw the results. People often say to me that I did not have to wait very long for Mick to become a Christian. It is true that he came to the Lord three months after me but, believe me, those months were the longest of my life. He had so much to say against God and Christianity, that I knew I had to keep my head down and keep praying. It was such a painful time for me: my faith was so young, and I was desperate to tell Mick how I felt about the Lord, but I knew not to, because it would incense him. I listened to him chuntering away about God. Every time we came out of church, he criticised the preacher and disputed the message. For the three-mile walk home, he ranted and I kept my peace. Every step I took, I called out to God to do something to change his heart. I had very little faith for Mick's salvation, but a great deal of sorrow for my marriage. I really thought that my love for Jesus would drive a wedge between Mick and myself, and it would be an end to our marriage. My fear drove me to pray without ceasing. I did not have any fellowship: I was a new Christian, and I did not have anyone to talk to about my dilemma. Happily, Nichola had an NIV Bible, which made everything so clear to me; I devoured it. Whilst I was interceding for Mick, so were Nichola and half of her church family. I thank God for drawing Mick to him when he did, because the intensity of the secrecy and prayer was quite a burden.

Having made his commitment to Jesus, Mick cried on and off for weeks. It really got on my nerves: everything reduced him to tears. I could not see a benefit of his faith for weeks: instead of an angry man, I had a sobbing wreck for a husband. I was such a young Christian that I did not realise that God was simply softening Mick's heart. Within a short time, Mick became a new man. The old hard, chain smoking, swearing Mick melted away. It was amazing. Attending church together as a family was wonderful, and we soon became involved in various ministries within the church. The Lord has revolutionised our family life, and our relationships with one another. Looking back, it really is hard to imagine what Mick used to be like. His hardness was nothing to God. God will be faithful and answer your prayers, too. Do not be discouraged if your husband is angry or disinterested; hang on in there, pray without ceasing for him —and you will get results; we did.

12

Steve Hayes

"In public I was a decent enough bloke. I was good company, and seemed to have a grip on life; but, deep inside, I was desperately unhappy."

My father died when I was three months old. We lived alone for the first nine years of my life, until my mother remarried. We were quite close, as she was such a very supportive woman, but she was not tactile; she never cuddled me or showed physical affection towards me. When she buried my father, my mother buried his memory with him. I do not remember her talking to me about him. I had no idea of how he had spoken or what he had looked like; nor did I discover anything about what his interests and talents had been. He was a distant figure, who had fathered me and then disappeared before I had the opportunity to develop a memory of him. Even my paternal grandmother never mentioned my natural father during her visits. As a result I was pretty 'closed down' emotionally.

My stepfather was a decent enough man, but we were never close. I think we became closer as I grew up, but I never had an intimate father-son relationship. Initially, I found having a stepfather very difficult, but I had no way of expressing how I felt as we simply did not connect on an emotional level at all. We all learnt how to live together harmoniously, yet we lacked the warmth that I recognised in other people's families. It was not something I thought about, simply accepting that was the way we were. I passed my '11 plus' examination and was therefore able to go to a good grammar school. I was content at school, and was bright, but not an academic 'high flyer'. I excelled on the sports field, which gave me adequate social standing amongst my peers and masked the fact that I lacked academic confidence. I would sit at the back of the class with my head in my hands, in fear that the teacher would ask me a question. Being singled out for any reason caused me acute embarrassment.

As part of our school curriculum, we had to attend daily Christian assemblies. These services were an absolute dirge, and had no reality to them. Christianity was presented as dull and lifeless; there was certainly no joy or hope attached to any of the messages I heard. No one suggested we should live our lives according to the Bible. I was confirmed as a boy, because we were told that was what was expected of us; there was no choice in the matter, so it meant little to me. I never thought deeply about God, due to the inability of the school to get a right and meaningful message across. Christianity held no attraction for me, so on leaving school I did not give it any further thought.

I decided not to go to university, but to take up a management apprenticeship with Lucas. I took various professional exams, which led me into personnel management. It was a curious career path for a person who battled constantly with a lack of confidence, but I loved the people, and the troubleshooting, problem solving side of the work. As I built up my professional confidence, I realised I could manage people effectively and was a good mediator and negotiator. My lack of confidence followed me into adulthood, but like many people I learnt an effective way to combat this. All it took was a couple of drinks to loosen my tongue, and I could social-ise with the rest of them!

Because I felt displaced, and longed for intimate attach-ment, I married at a young age. Shortly after we were mar-ried, my stepfather was killed in a horrendous car accident. My mother was seriously injured and spent six months in hospital. Looking back, I realise I was totally unmoved at my stepfather's funeral, because I did not believe in an afterlife. It was simply a ritual of ending, holding no truth or special meaning for me; it was something we simply went through, in order to finalise one chapter and start another. During that time, I was left to run the family business. It was an ex-tremely dark time for us all. I coped with it by doing what I had to do, aided and abetted by the odd stiff drink. Mum did not share her pain of losing her husband and, once again, emotions were buried. On the few occasions we went to church for weddings and christenings, nothing ever touched me, and I certainly never had any inclination to seek God, nor to read the Bible. It never entered my head that I could talk to God or draw strength from him.

Life was busy for us. I was working hard in the motor industry and soon became a senior manager. We had two chil-dren and, like most men, I became absorbed in being the 'hunter gatherer'. I worked long hours, which often included my lunch break, and poured all my energy into my work. I relaxed by playing golf, which, though it kept me sane, af-fected our family life. Throughout our marriage we had many trials and tribulations and, after seventeen years or so, we were in serious trouble in our relationship. We plodded on for several more years, but eventually things deteriorated to an irreparable state. Sadly, we were unable to reconcile our dif-ferences, and divorced when our two children were in their late teens. Whilst going through this process, I was made re-dundant.

It is fair to say that I was thoroughly miserable and, not for the first time in my life, I felt displaced. Many of my friends turned their backs against me, and I found myself being

drawn into comfort drinking. It seemed such an effective way
to blot out pain. It did not dawn on me that I was being completely ineffective in sorting out my life. I was perfectly capable of resolving major industrial disputes involving hundreds of people; crossing picket lines; negotiating with people from all walks of life with opposing views; yet, in my personal life, I was completely useless. I became a professional
ostrich; my head was permanently in the sand, rather than
facing up to painful situations and emotions.

Over the years, like many people, I became a regular
drinker. With hindsight, I feel that I could have become
more than a social drinker, had I not met Lesley and become
a Christian. In public I was a 'decent enough bloke'. I was
good company and seemed to have a grip on life, but deep
inside I was desperately unhappy.

I remember having a medical check-up at that time. I had
a battery of tests, and afterwards the doctor asked me if I was
drinking more than 21 units per week. I told her I was, but
explained I was going through a divorce, moving house, and
moving job. She asked me a few more questions and said,
"Well, just don't let anything else happen to you, Steve, because you are dealing with three major life events at the moment, and we don't want you to die." It is curious that I remember that. I was not frightened by her words, because I
had little regard for my own wellbeing; she simply confirmed
I had a great deal to contend with. Perhaps in some way her
response seemed to justify my alcohol intake. I am ashamed
to say I occasionally drank too much and took unnecessary
risks with my safety that I would never consider doing in the
cold light of day. I know now that God must have had his
hand on me even in those days. Without my realising it, God
saw my innermost pain and knew how to reach me, even
though I did not know how to reach him.

During the darkest time of my life, I met Lesley who, for
some inexplicable reason, saw something in me that I could
not see in myself. Like me, she had divorced from an unhappy marriage, but she seemed to be coping with life much
better than me. Lesley and I deepened our relationship; she

was so easy to love, as she is such a beautiful, caring, gentle woman. I loved being with her, and respected that religion was important to her, happily attending church services with her from time to time. I was not at all threatened by her faith; she was not the type of woman to 'make a song and dance' about things. She was quite relaxed about religion, so I had no need to feel threatened; if she was happy, then so was I. We frequently went to early morning services in Worcester Cathedral, which attracted some excellent speakers. They were lively, interesting and, most importantly, their messages were relevant to everyday living. Looking back over my life, I can see clearly that there were several significant people I met, who somehow seemed to be steering me towards God. It was as though they were each holding open separate doors, which would lead to a final rendezvous with God. Many of the speakers in Worcester Cathedral were amongst those 'doorkeepers'.

We married and moved, with my new job, to Wales. By our third wedding anniversary we had moved to Leamington, where Lesley started attending a community church. This was very different to the church services we had attended previously. Since we first met, Lesley had made it very clear to me that God was important to her, so, when she announced she had 'asked Jesus into her life', I was intrigued. She ex-plained that, all her life, she felt that having a relationship with God was about earning approval, being a good person, and notching up 'brownie points' to get a bit closer to him. The church she now attended taught her that was not the case, but that we are accepted and loved by God unconditionally, through accepting Jesus Christ into our lives. Lesley encouraged me to attend some of the services with her, and it was there that God put two more 'doorkeepers' across my path. Paul Downes and Royston Young had a profound influ-ence on me. Paul was one of those men who manage to fit forty eight hours into each day without getting stressed. He was so energetic and lively, and clearly had a tremendous faith in God. Royston was a lecturer at the university. I had met plenty of intelligent, eloquent, confident men in my time, but this man was different. His whole demeanour was so appealing. He was such a peaceful man, and I admired the way he had no difficulty showing his thoughtfulness and kindness to people. He was openly loving towards everyone he met, and his ability to connect with people so easily was stunning. I had never been able to physically demonstrate how I felt about people, and was curious to know why he could be so open whilst I could not. The nearest I got to being passionate about anything was reducing my golf handicap! Royston and I became friends, and I felt comfortable in his company; so when he invited me to attend a small group at his home, I agreed to go. It was similar to the *Alpha* groups we run now, and we started exploring the Bible together. Our meetings were non-threatening and non-invasive: we simply talked about God. I clearly remember Royston suggesting that I read the first chapter of John's Gospel. Because I respected him and wanted to understand what the difference was between us, I followed that advice. The chapter clearly pointed out who Jesus was, and why he came to earth.

In the beginning was the Word and the Word was with God, and the Word was God. He was with God in the beginning. Through him, all things were made; without him nothing was made that has been made. In him was life, and that life was the light of men. The light shines in the darkness, but the darkness has not understood it. There came a man who was sent by God; his name was John. He came as a witness to testify concerning that light, so that through him all men might believe. He himself was not the light; he came only as a witness to the light. The true light that gives light to every man was coming into the world.

John 1:1–10

I read the chapter over and over, until it made sense to me. Without my realising it, the words began to touch my heart, and came to mean a great deal to me. Around that time Lesley announced that, now she had truly found the Lord, she wanted to be baptised. I did not understand why, as I knew she had been christened as an infant; but I happily supported her, and went along to her baptism. She seemed so happy, which made me happy for her. Secretly, I started to question my own spirituality, but I did not tell Lesley. Shortly after that, I started to learn a little about the Holy Spirit. We studied Galatians 5, comparing life with and without the Holy Spirit. In this passage, the apostle Paul calls us to be imitators of God. According to Paul, it should be evident from a person's behaviour whether he has the Lord in his life or not.

The acts of the sinful nature are obvious: sexual immorality, impurity and debauchery; idolatry and witchcraft; hatred, discord, jealousy, fits of rage, selfish ambition, dissensions, factions and envy; drunkenness, orgies and the like. I warn you, as I did before, that those who live like this will not inherit the kingdom of God.

Galatians 5:19–21

Having read that passage, it dawned on me that many of those things had applied to my life over the years, to some degree or another; and I was distinctly uncomfortable with this. I read that love, joy, peace, patience, kindness, goodness, gentleness, faithfulness and self-control were all characteristics of having our lives right with the Lord. Comparing what I was like with what I should be like was enormously challenging; and I started to understand what the difference was between my life and Royston's. Lesley and I attended a talk given by Mary Pytches, in which she talked about God wanting to remodel our lives. Suddenly, I understood what she meant, and her words clearly influenced my desire to reorder my life. I knew I was not the man God intended me to be, but I feared the change would be too high a price for me to pay. It started to dawn on me that I had never been fatherless: my heavenly Father knew me inside out, and had never left me for one moment. In Romans chapter 5, I read that faith brought joy, and I now understood that, over the years, God had gently led me into his presence, and I had a decision to make. There was little outward sign of the activity in my spiritual life; most of the action took place quietly, out of sight, in the very depths of my soul. It must have been so hard for Lesley, as I know she longed for dramatic outward signs that something was happening; but the Lord respected my need for a gentle walk with him.

I went with Lesley to a Christmas carol service, and realised that I believed that Jesus was the Son of God; and quietly, in the silence of my heart, asked Jesus if I could have access to his life, and he to mine. I really do not remember feeling different, except that I knew I was ready to trust God with my life. A few weeks later, I decided to go through a believer's baptism, and it was before that service that I publicly said the prayer of commitment, and knew without a shadow of doubt that I could feel God's presence in my life.

The amazing thing about God is that he meets us where we are. He knows I am not the kind of man who would have coped with a 'big production' conversion; he gently led me to a place of intimacy with him. There was no great fanfare or fuss; he simply took me by the hand, and we gently walked together into his throne room.

I began to meet people within the church who began to bring the reality of the Bible into my life; their lives impinged on mine in a very positive way. I found myself reflecting on my past life, and saw a definite pattern that, during my darkest time, I had been 'carried'. Someone gave me a copy of the poem *Footprints*, and suddenly I could relate to those words. Even though I did not know the Lord, he knew me and never left me —not once. I had gradually developed a simple faith through the gentle witness of people I had met. I had not had a dramatic prayer conversion moment, like many of those whose testimonies are recorded in this book. It was as if I gently slid into God's arms.

Because I did not grow up with a father, it has been

difficult for me to relate to my heavenly Father. Now, suddenly, I had the Father I had never had. Working in 'people management', I have been a personnel director in fairly large companies. I am now an independent manager-consultant, which gives me access to huge numbers of people in my working life. I have always enjoyed working with people, and have always tried to deal with issues sensitively, ensuring that people are dealt with fairly and properly. Having dealt with incredibly difficult situations, from industrial disputes to major factory closures, I feel I have always acted with integrity, but, now that I am a Christian, my faith has reinforced my understanding of fair trading, and has given me added confidence, with the knowledge that I am not the major decision maker, in life—God is.

I had been brought up to believe that people in senior positions were to be respected, and that because of their position in life, were pretty special because of that. I admired those who were high achievers or were successful —not necessarily in a materialistic way: I was not over impressed by anyone because of their car or big house. But I had revered great sportsmen and businessmen. These days, I look at the person, rather than what they do or achieve; a person's heart and integrity are far better indicators of success than their possessions and positions in life.

I firmly believe that I would not have become a Christian if I had not met Lesley; yet in some way, looking back over my journey, it was almost as if I were predestined to meet with God. I can see clearly that his hand had been on mine throughout my life. He placed some wonderful 'doorkeepers' in my path, to lead me through my journey to him. Had I continued to live as I was, I would have been heading for a mighty fall, leading a totally hedonistic lifestyle. Many people have addictions to mask pain; alcohol, drugs and relationships are but a few examples of such things. It is an easy trap to fall into, and I thank God he spared me from that. Golf has always been a passion in my life (it is a great game), but I had used it as a distraction, not just as a healthy pastime. I had been able to carve out a pocket of peace, and hide away for hours at a time—but it was transient. The moment I put my clubs away, my problems returned.

Since putting God into his rightful place in my life, we have still had a fair number of trials. We realised that we had both brought a great deal of 'baggage' into our marriage from our previous relationships, and the effects were beginning to have an impact. I am sure that without the Lord in our lives our relationship would not have survived. Through God's infinite gentleness, and wise counsel from Christian friends, our marriage is strong and healthy; and I will be eternally grateful to Lesley for seeing so much good in me. When we met, my life was a mess. Lesley knew that she could not, on her own, restore the balance to my life, but she knew someone who could. My wife led me to the Lord —and, ultimately, a better life. I know, without a shadow of doubt, that a major turning point was reading John's Gospel. I encourage anyone who is interested in finding out more about God (and challenge those who are not interested) to read it. It was a key for me, and I cannot see that it would be any different for anybody else. The word of God is valid and relevant to everyday situations; read it and see!

We belong to a vibrant church, and I am so happy to be there, but initially I was terrified, as I felt so intimidated by the outward expression of love for God and each other. I think Christian wives need to be sensitive to that. In every walk of life we usually choose to be with like-minded people to whom we can relate; it is important that this happens within the church, too, and that one finds a church where a seeker will be welcome. As long as it is a Bible believing church, committed to preaching the word, and that it takes people into a deeper relationship with Jesus, it does not matter whether you wave incense or wave your arms —it is the fruit of the Spirit that is important.

Life is now a million times better than it used to be before I knew Jesus Christ as my personal Lord and Saviour — and it is getting better all the time. I love the Scriptures and I am committed to 'friendship evangelism', which must be natural, not forced. After all, it worked for me! Although we have been through several periods of unemployment, be-reavement, relocation and the usual trials of family life, we have been sustained by the grace of God in our spiritual and emotional lives; and have come through our problems stronger than we had been before.

I now appreciate what Mary Pytches was saying to me, all those years ago: God longed to 'remodel' my life. I am so thankful that I allowed him to do so. The Lord often brings opportunities to me to show his love for other people. That is something of which I would have been incapable in my own strength. I had, genuinely, feared the cost of becoming com-mitted to God. I thought he would want all my time and money. What a joke that is: he has given me far more than I deserve, and I could never begin to give him a fraction of what I owe him.

Lesley and I have been involved in *Alpha*, as I feel it is important to reach out to people, and to lay the facts before them. Because I struggled to find God and failed miserably, partly because I was not in the right church, I feel passion-ately that it is important for us to make the journey to faith of others as easy as possible. I clearly remember the people in my life who had the 'wow factor'; the men who captivated my attention because of the authority they commanded, and I would like to see more men's evangelism. Christian men who are successful in their careers or sporting achievements have a great deal of public appeal, and can open up chinks of curi-osity in the non-believer, which opens up ways for the Lord to move in their lives. We should use their testimonies to attract a wider male audience into our churches.

I still play my beloved golf, by the way, but I enjoy it purely as a sport —not as a form of escape, as I did for so many years. I am far more confident and outgoing, so I think God has done a pretty fine job of beginning to 'remodel' me so far....

It took me a lot longer than Lesley to take on board God's message to me; but I got there eventually, and so will your husband —in God's time. I cannot urge you women enough to *keep on praying* for your husband; trust God, be patient, and have faith that you and your household will be saved.

13

Lesley Hayes

However, as it is written: "...No eye has seen, no ear has heard, no mind has conceived what God has prepared for those who love him" —but God has revealed it to us by his Spirit.

I Cor 2:9–10

My upbringing was quite different from Steve's. I had kind, dedicated parents, who loved me, but I always felt that part of their love for me was conditional upon my behaviour. They were obviously so pleased with me when I did well at school that I grew up with the idea that God also judged my achievements, and it was my duty to *perform* well in life to earn his approval. We attended church as a family, and religion was integral to our home life. I loved singing, and belonged to a church choir. My confirmation, at the age of fourteen, meant a great deal to me. During the service I felt I really had a spiritual encounter with God. I was in real fear of the Lord, and brought myself up very strictly, denying myself a lot of the pleasures other girls of my age seemed to embrace. I knew what the Old Testament said about God, but I had no real understanding of Jesus. The teaching I received was

based upon 'respecting God', but Jesus was not the key figure in my faith. I strived to be a good person, in order to be
acceptable to God; sadly, no one ever explained to me where
Jesus 'fits in'. I honestly believed that if I were to lead a good
life and strive to be good, then I would be okay. I had been
involved in hundreds of services —and missed the whole
point. What I failed to understand at that time was that God
wants to be involved in everything, including the issue of
whether I should marry, and whom I should marry. I simply
had not been taught that. I feared God, but did not realise
that I was special in his eyes, nor that he longed for a relationship with me. I had no idea I could talk to him about everything that was happening in my life, just as I would to a
friend. I struggled on my own, simply because I had no idea
I could have a two-way relationship with God. I really believe
I could have saved myself a lot of grief over the years, had I
known that simple fact.

I married in my mid twenties, but my husband was not a
believer, which was very sad for me, as we did not share an
important part of my life —my religion. We had a difficult
nine years before separating, and following my divorce I secretly vowed to myself that, if ever I remarried, my husband
would have to at least be interested in God and be open to my
faith. I was involved with church life, and felt that it should
be an integral part of any relationship I might have in the
future. When I met Steve, he was in such a mess after his
divorce he was a bit of a 'displaced' soul, and I was oblivious
to the fact that unresolved issues from our first marriages
would have a 'knock-on' effect in our relationship. Steve and
I were in love, and I naively thought that protected us from
making more mistakes.

From the outset, I made it very clear to Steve how important my faith was to me. The lovely thing was that he was
really happy for me to attend church, and would often go with
me. The frustration for me came when I realised that golf
was a major part in Steve's life. He spent hours on the golf
course, and I felt that both God and I were competing for his
time and attention. I could not see how I could get Steve off

the golf course and into church more regularly —it seemed too big a task. I so wanted him to get the balance of his life right, for both our sakes. I do not think I can say he was overwhelmed by the way I lived. I did not exude peace and contentment, as many Christians do. In some ways, I was not easy to live with. I was far from relaxed. As a working mother, life was frantic for me. My fast pace of life was reflected in my behaviour —I was *driven*. I worked full time, which often involved driving 1000 miles a week. By that time I had two children, and I would never consider making life easier for myself by serving a ready made meal. Everything had to be done to a high standard. I had a lot of unlearning to do: the Lesley who had to prove herself all the time took some time to wise up to the fact that she did not have to be 'superwoman'. Instead of settling down into married life and enjoying our children, we had the aftermath of our divorces to cope with. Although I experienced enormous love and warmth from Steve, I was far from being a peaceful person. At the time, I had no idea that we had taken so much 'baggage' into our marriage; and sailed on, oblivious to the effect it was having on our relationship. On my part, I did not love myself; my self-esteem was low, and I could not imagine how anyone could love me. That would come later, after I had the Lord in my life, had received wise counsel —and buckets of God's infinite love.

Getting involved with the church in Leamington was such an enlightening experience for me. The services were vibrant, and there was a freedom in worship that I had not experienced before. I was so ready for a deeper relationship with the Lord. I welcomed this new type of service with open arms. For the first time in my life, I heard that the Lord wanted an intimate relationship with me. I realised I had been living under false pretences; God's love for me was absolutely unconditional. I did not have to be a 'straight A' student, or get a first class honours degree, to count as special in his eyes. He loved me for who I was. I came to realise that there was a way to reach God's heart —and that was through Jesus, not through my good works and good intentions.

I remember how I was hoovering our bedroom, mulling over some of the teaching I had heard at church. The sun was streaming in through our huge bedroom window. The warmth from the sun seemed so intense, so powerful, that I stopped what I was doing and soaked up the heat of the rays. It was such a special moment: I knew, in that instant, that the warmth I felt was a reflection of God's love for me —I knew he wanted to bathe me in the warmth of his love. I knew that he had loved me through all the times I had messed up; and in that moment I knew what I had to do to personalise my relationship with him. I knelt down in the stream of sunshine and asked the Lord into my life. In that moment I experienced the incredible intensity of God's love for me. In an instant I found the missing link to my relationship with the Lord. I had been to church every week of my life, and had been denied access to the most amazing intimacy with God. One vital ingredient had been missing: the right teaching. No one had taught me that I could have unconditional access to the living God. Suddenly, I understood that my wrong kind of fear, and what I supposed to be 'reverence' for God, had blocked out the warmth of his love in my life. I could not wait to share my experience with Steve. Because he was not a demonstrative man, he seemed to have problems processing what had happened to me. Thankfully, because he loved me he was happy for me, and continued to come along to church with me. That evening, I announced to our house group that I had at last put my life right with the Lord; they, of course, were delighted. Six weeks later, I was baptised, and was encouraged to pray for the in-filling of the Holy Spirit. From that day, I have never looked back.

Having realised what I had been missing out on all my life, I was desperate for Steve to share my experience, too. It was beyond me why he could not see that what I was saying was the truth. All I was asking him to do was to open his heart to something that was even better than he had already. I was not offering him something that should come with a government health warning: it was not poisonous or harmful, but something which would enrich his life. It was a frustrating time for me, and it took me a little while to learn that I had to leave my frustrations with God, and love Steve despite his attitude. In a way, I had to love him twice as much.

As the weeks passed, my frustration with Steve gathered momentum. I could not see any outward sign of him getting closer to the Lord; nothing seemed to be happening. How desperately I longed for him to experience the love of Jesus in his life, and to 'force' him into faith. Sometimes I wanted to take him by the collar and shake him like a rag doll —until he understood what I meant! I was so excited to have found a personal relationship with Jesus. It had been such an incredibly liberating experience to realise that God was not a stern, judgemental being after all; I was fit to burst. Steve's inability to believe was beyond me, and it was so tempting to try and make him come off the fence to make a decision about God. Thankfully, the leaders of our church explained to me that everyone comes to God in a unique way; that I had to learn to *trust in the Lord* that my husband would be born again; and that it was in the Lord's time and, just as importantly, in *his* way —not mine. They encouraged me not to plot and plan Steve's conversion, but to pray without ceasing for him, and to give him space to find God at his pace, not mine.

So I took their advice, and mounted a prayer campaign. I called out to the Lord to remove the obstacles of unbelief from Steve, and I enlisted as much help as I could. I was determined to do all I could, and met regularly with friends, to pray for him. If nagging could not do the trick, then I was sure prayer could. The church leadership were infinitely patient with me, and taught me to hand my concerns over to Jesus —and not take them back. Worrying, mothering and nagging would only have a detrimental effect, hindering Steve's journey to faith. I now appreciate that their wise counsel was invaluable, as I have heard of so many women who go through agony, trying to convert their husbands. It is something we cannot do —only the Lord can.

Steve often came to church with me, but I attended house group on my own, as he simply was not ready for that level of commitment. Whilst initially disappointed that he did not want to come with me, I now see that time as an opportunity for the people in the group to be a huge blessing and support to me. Because Steve was not with me, they had the freedom to nurture my faith for his conversion. They went on encouraging me not to be impatient with his lack of faith. Above all, they joined with me in praying for him: we spent hours calling out to God for him.

During this time I would often wake during the night, and would pray for Steve as he slept. I knew that God could open the eyes of his heart, and I called out to him to do that. Two of the church leaders got on exceptionally well with him, and basically took on the role of friendship evangelists. They often went out for a curry together, and during their 'curry nights' the conversation inevitably came around to God, and they simply 'drip-fed' him the truth. They befriended him, answered his questions, and had a good time together. Meanwhile, I was praying frantically for him. My desperation for him to know the amazing love which I had discovered increased, and I took my task of 'praying without ceasing' very seriously.

After I had asked Jesus into my life, I learnt about believer's baptism, and was baptised in Leamington Church. Steve came along to the service, which was a wonderful event for me; but I was disappointed that there were no visible signs that he was becoming more interested in the Lord. Little did I know that most of the action was taking place very deep inside his heart. I only had to wait another three months before Steve realised what I had been raving on about! I began to grow as a Christian, and felt very peaceful about sharing what was happening to me with him. I felt strongly that I should not hide things from him simply because he did not understand what was happening to me. I had chosen Steve, to share my life with him, and accepted that, even though he was not at the stage I was at, it would be dishonourable not to be open with him. We would often discuss sermons and house group meetings. I usually initiated the conversations, but it seemed so important not to ignore what was happening, nor to 'compartmentalise' it as something that did not involve him. I did not at that time realise that one of his greatest fears of becoming committed was the cost to self. He was frightened that he would have to give up his beloved golf, and give most of his money away to the church; it was all, understandably, far too threatening for him. I felt that Steve was prevaricating —whilst, all the time, the Lord was gently easing him into a trusting position with him. It seemed incredible to me that Steve could settle disputes involving thousands of people, and yet he could not sort out a dispute between himself and God.

Finally, after a great deal of intensive prayer, teaching and loving friendship from within the church, Steve asked Jesus into his life. He, too, wanted to be baptised, which was a wonderful experience for us all. Then, now that we had both become Christians, we suddenly became aware of the cracks in our marriage, and went through a few stormy times repairing the damage. We had had no idea that our relationship needed some major repair work, and that we had to work through the 'baggage' we had brought into our marriage from previous relationships. I know, without a shadow of doubt, that we would not have survived without having become Christians. Thankfully, God saw that, and showed us a very different way to lead our lives. I can honestly say that the Lord swept us both up at the right time; it was a bit like being rescued from a sinking ship. Sharing faith in Jesus did not suddenly turn us into a fairy tale couple, but it has helped us to evolve into much better people; and we now have a wonderful marriage. I am still quite often a 'golf widow', and battle with the fact that, during the summer months, Steve spends hours away from the family. However, I respond differently to that, these days. Rather than being resentful about the time he spends on the golf course, I now appreciate that golf keeps him fit; he is out in the fresh air, and often he is able to minister the love of Jesus to many of the men who are deeply unhappy but, as he once did, pretend they have life sorted out.

My advice is to pray without ceasing for your husband, and love him unconditionally. We choose to share our lives with these men of ours. Be patient with them, be sensitive, but do not be secretive; and seek wise counsel from your church leaders. Remember to continually cover your husband and children in a blanket of prayer. It worked for us!

Conclusion

The stories you have read are not uncommon; they are representative of what God has done, and longs to do more of, throughout the world. Our men belong in church with us. I believe the Lord is doing a new thing; he wants to stir his children to pray without ceasing for their loved ones, and see husbands and wives united in his love.

You may be the only 'copy' of the Bible your husband reads. Behave honourably; and be as loving, supportive and caring towards him as you can. His days are numbered: he will be born again, but you have to learn that it will be in God's time, not yours. No amount of nagging, arranged meetings, tracts or pleading will speed up the process. Be patient with your husband's lack of faith, and pray for him. Pray that God will bless him, and pray that he will reveal his perfect will in your husband's life. God can see the exact date, hour and second your husband will bow the knee to him. Learn not to waste precious time and energy crying, 'When, Lord?' —because we already know his reply is: 'In my time.' Be patient! Instead, try concentrating on blessing your husband on a daily basis, both in prayer and in your loving actions.

Your husband has been forced to share his life with the

Lord—someone he does not believe in, nor want to know. He eats with, wakes up with, and communes with Jesus, every day of his life, simply because **Jesus is in you**. Be patient with his unbelief. All you need is faith as big as a mustard seed. With the Lord's infinite love, patience and wisdom, you can move mountains. God is calling out to you to take up the mantle of intercession for your husband. Will you respond?

Just imagine the Lord sitting opposite you right now. He leans forward, looks you gently in the eye, and tells you he has a special ministry for you. It is not a ministry that will take you to exotic locations or give you public recognition; but it is a ministry that he very much wants to see fulfilled.

Imagine Jesus telling you that, since the beginning of time, you were the one person in the whole of creation that he chose for this job. Your first reaction would probably be that he had made a mistake; surely you could not be the only person in the whole of creation; and, as you look up into his face to tell him how you feel... he looks deeply into your eyes. In an instant, you know that you are his chosen one, and you know you can do as he asks —simply because he has asked.

Jesus tells you he would like you to tend a seed for him; a special seed that is capable of bearing wonderful fruit; that will bring him and you absolute pleasure. How do you think you would respond to his voice, his gaze, his request? Now imagine him placing a tiny seed in the palm of your hand. It is so fragile that you fear it will blow away if you breathe too heavily on it. He tells you that you must grow the plant outdoors, where it will be exposed to the elements and potential dangers; but he will provide all the resources you could possibly need, and he will be on call twenty four hours a day, seven days a week, to offer you advice and support. How precious would you feel in the presence of Almighty God at that moment? Would any of us refuse his request?

Assuming you accept the assignment, how would you make sure you did the best possible job you could? I know I would use every resource available to me, to ensure I did not let Jesus down. I would devour every gardening book I could get my hands on. I would seek the advice of experienced, reputable gardeners, and soak myself in knowledge. I would buy the best plant food I could afford, and the strongest stake to hold the growing plant in place. I would protect it from pests and fungi, and I would even get up in the middle of the night to protect my plant from the elements.

I would be the best gardener I could possibly be, at all times. I would regularly check with the Lord that I was doing okay, and seek his advice as to how to deal with any problems I might encounter. I would commit myself to my godly, appointed role, until my plant bore the beautiful fruit that the Lord promised me.

So often in the Bible, Jesus talks to us in gardening terms when referring to spiritual growth. It is an analogy that many people understand. Every time I pray about this book, the Lord shows me a rich harvest of men. I was so taken with what the Lord was saying that, for the first time in my life, I went out and bought a packet of cress seeds. When I opened the pack, I was struck by their appearance. According to the blurb, they were guaranteed to be edible in eight days. To my mind, that seemed impossible: they looked so lifeless. Yet, within hours of putting them in the right conditions, they start to bear life. Most of the activity will go unnoticed, but the growth continues... despite our lack of awareness. And that is exactly how it is with your husband's faith. You might not think there is a lot of activity in his spiritual life, but believe me, once you start to pray, there will be.

Think of your husband's journey of faith as that tiny seed. Before it can bear fruit, there has to be a great deal of hard work. Most of it will be down to you; but you are *not* a lone gardener. The resources available to you are infinite. You have Jesus, the master gardener, to call upon, day and night! He who created all things will lead you in all your ways. Each of you will spend different amounts of time tending the seed, and each of you will have a different way of doing this. But the wonderful thing about the Lord is that he treats us as individuals, and he will show you how to tend your husband's journey of faith. It is not going to be the same as my journey, nor that of your best friends. The rate of growth will vary for all of you; some will have longer than others to wait, but one thing I am absolutely sure of is that God has no favourites, and what he did for my husband, he will do for yours. It does not matter where you are in your relationship with your husband at this moment in time; it is your relationship with the Lord that matters.

Maybe you are chomping at the bit, and cannot wait to get down to prayer for your husband, or maybe you have become tired or disinterested; wherever you are, Jesus knows, and he is prepared to meet you now, and take you forward. Are you prepared to commit to nurture your husband's faith? Today is a brand new day: the Lord's blessings are new every morning; use today as a fresh start for yourself and your husband.

So how and where do we start? First of all, you have to prepare the ground and rid it of weeds and stones. You do this by presenting yourself before God with clean hands and a pure heart. You may need to ask Jesus to forgive you for your attitude towards your husband, and then move on. For some, this may be a simple prayer, but for others it may need deeper ministry. But if you do not prepare *yourself* you will jeopardise your ministry to your husband.

Secondly, you dig a trench, sow the seed and cover with earth. Using the word of God to claim your husband into faith is essential for this part. My favourite scripture is Acts 16:31. Simply pray,

Father, in Acts 16, your word says, 'You and your household' will be saved. So I ask you now, in the name of Jesus, that you will honour this scripture and save my husband. I pray that he will be born again of the Spirit of God, in Jesus' name. Amen.

Next you must 'water' continuously, with specific prayers. For instance, ask the Holy Spirit to reveal to you anything in your husband's life or ancestry that is holding him back. This could be, for example, fear, stubbornness, arrogance, freemasonry or the occult.

Father I ask that you will draw............ close to you this day. Release him from anything that is holding him back. Through the power of your Holy Spirit, show me how to pray for him. Lift the veil of unbelief from his spirit and reveal Jesus to him. In Jesus' name I pray. Amen.

We also protect from damage and disease by praying blessings on our husbands. You could use one of the doxologies for this, such as the following:

'The Lord bless you and keep you, the Lord cause his face to shine upon you and be gracious unto you, and give you his peace.'

I always personalise scripture by inserting the person's name I am praying for, (i.e. 'The Lord bless you and keep you, Robert Forrester, etc., etc.') The other simple way I used to pray was to bless the place where Rob sat and slept; each time I made the bed I always prayed...

Father, I ask that you will bless this place of rest. Every time Robert lays his head on this pillow, please reveal Jesus to him. I ask that your angels will minister the love of Jesus to him as he sleeps. In Jesus' name. Amen.

Finally, we fertilise the plant with buckets of love. You do this simply by providing for your husband's needs in a loving, caring manner. Make him feel special, and show him how much you appreciate him and need his support. Occasionally, a little specialist care might be needed, and fasting and prayer may be appropriate, as the Lord leads you.

Eventually, when the time is right, we harvest the fruit. The Lord will have that in hand; it may be you who leads your husband to faith, or it may be someone else. Believe me, when it comes to harvest time, you will not mind who the harvester is!

I have heard many testimonies of husbands who have come to faith, and I am convinced of two things. Firstly, **God does not lie, and he can see the date your husband will come to faith**; and, secondly, the women who prayed for their husbands **trusted totally in God's faithfulness**. I do not have a guaranteed formula to bring your husband to faith, but I do have absolute faith that he will come to know the Lord.

In order to be a good gardener, you need knowledge and skills —which the Lord will gladly equip you with. Your essential tool kit consists of prayer, Bible study, fellowship and *more prayer*. Be the best wife you can be, and enjoy tending your precious ministry.

I thought you might find it helpful for me to identify some of the things which men have told me helped and hindered their journey to faith. Each man I have written about is unique; turning points and key events differ enormously, but all agreed one thing: **you are a living example of what Jesus has to offer**. That you may be the only Bible your husband is reading is an awesome thought. But the good news is that the Lord is in control of your ministry.... He has already drawn up the care plans for your husband, and can see exactly what lies ahead. He has already allocated all the resources you could possibly need. The best news of all is that he can see the date your husband will come to faith.

I look forward to hearing of the rich harvest which God has promised you for your husband.

'Turn offs'

- Lengthy telephone calls, day and night, to Christians
- Littering the place with books and Christian music
- Talking God all the time
- Always at church or meetings
- Arranging 'chance' meetings with Christian friends
- Bible bashing
- Swearing
- Giving up common interests
- Moaning
- Criticising church and Christians
- Flirting
- Bad behaviour
- Becoming angry with husband's lack of faith
- Being ashamed of non-Christian husband in front of Christian friends

'Turn ons'

- Being calm and loving
- Peaceful home
- Having time for husband
- Good behaviour
- Discreet about faith
- Being home at night
- Taking phone calls when husband is out of the house
- Continuing with joint interests
- Laughing together
- Being friends
- Making husband feel he is still important
- Practising what you preach
- Making non Christian friends welcome

You might like to use the following as a checklist:

- Prepare self; forgive — move on
- Present yourself before God with clean hands and pure heart
- Claim husband — pray in scripture
- Daily prayers and blessings
- Support other Christians
- Intercession: personal and group
- Check your behaviour
- Thank the Lord for what he is doing and has promised to do
- Fasting

These are some of the prayers the women in our church pray regularly for their husbands. The prayers are not restricted by copyright, and may be reproduced.

Father, in the name of Jesus, I ask that you will cleanse my home, from the rooftop to the foundations, with the blood of the Lamb. Cleanse it of anything that is not of you, including all music, television programmes, media, conversations and other influences. Fill my home with your Holy Spirit and your ministering angels, Lord. In Jesus' name, I pray. Amen.

Father, I ask that you will draw............ close to you this day. Lift the veil of unbelief from his spirit, and reveal Jesus to him. In Jesus' name, I pray. Amen.

Father, I ask that you will bless this place of rest. Everytime .... lays his head on this pillow, please reveal Jesus to him. I ask that your angels will minister the love of Jesus to him as he sleeps. In Jesus' name. Amen.

Jesus, you say, "Come to me, all who are weary and burdened, and I will give you rest."[1] Well, Lord, I feel worn out; please lift my burden from me, and give me your energy to pray without ceasing for my husband. In Jesus' name. Amen.

Jesus, I cannot see too much growth in my husband's life at the moment, but you can see everything, and I trust in your unfailing love for him and me. Thank you that he will be saved. Amen.

I can think of no finer words with which to finish this book than those of the apostle Paul:

Finally, brothers, whatever is true, whatever is noble, whatever is right, whatever is pure, whatever is lovely, whatever is admirable—if anything is excellent or praiseworthy—think about such things. Whatever you have learned or received or heard from me, or seen in me—put it into practice. And the God of peace will be with you.

Philippians 4:8–9

Please contact me at:
www.whenjesuswins.com

---

[1] Matt. 11:28